Remember Providence

Simone Varney

Published by Simone Varney, 2024.

Table of Contents

To my dear friend Katharine.

You always believed.

AUTHOR'S NOTE

I think it's important to explain how I approached telling my story. I cannot claim to have a perfect memory, or to be the arbiter of truth. This is how I experienced the things that happened, what I thought about them, and how I believe I responded in the moment and across time. I have no intention of telling other people's stories, so without altering mine, I have tried to hide the who's who of those I interacted with. I've changed names, timing, and misdirected by altering details that didn't affect the story.

AUTHOR'S NOTE

I think it's important to explain how I approached telling my story. I cannot claim to have a perfect memory, or to be the arbiter of truth. This is how I experienced the things that happened, what I thought about them, and how I believe I responded in the moment and across time. I have no intention of telling other people's stories, so without altering mine, I have tried to hide the who's who of those I interacted with. I've changed names, timing, and misdirected by altering details that didn't affect the story.

Mere Beginnings

Early 1980s

The man stared. He meant something by it, his eyes pulling like he had the Force on his side. People trailed across the Wharenui (communal house on the marae) between us, their bare feet a muffled thunder on the floor, and I followed their movement before turning back to the man. Two people in the trail stopped to chat, blocking his view, breaking his grip. I felt its absence and edged left and right, craning my neck, trying to find him again. Our eyes met, his nod telling me things were proceeding just as he expected. He double flicked his head, raising his eyebrows like the boys from school did, and I knew that meant he wanted me to come over. I took a few steps before stopping to scan the room for my parents, but they were nowhere to be seen.

The man leant forward in his seat. "Come 'ere," he mouthed. I followed his instruction, slicing through the line of people, and he straightened and patted his knee. I sat lightly, hands in my lap, eyes trained on them. Then I felt the pressure, something being asked of me, no words, just expectancy. I held still in case movement suggested something I didn't mean. Then I felt his arm rest around my waist and saw the act had caught the attention of those nearby. I stole a glance at him from under my fringe.

"You're the teacher's daughter," he said, stating the obvious, as I was the only Pākehā (non-Māori (white) New Zealander) girl in

1

the village, blonde hair, blue eyes, freckles. "Do you like this?" he said, indicating my seat on his lap. When I nodded, the corner of his mouth rose slightly, and I smiled. I figured it was now my turn, but I didn't know what to say. Fortunately, several other young teens arrived in the doorway opposite, scrambling for position, searching the room, and when they spotted me, it was clear they'd found what they were looking for. I'd been playing Spotlight outside with them earlier, so I pushed off the man's knee and half ran towards them before being slowed by a heavy feeling in my stomach. I spun round to see the man's head belatedly catching me up, dark eyes settling on mine as he leant back in the chair and blew out forcefully. My fellow teens were still waiting, watching as this real-life soap opera played out. I forced myself to head towards them, and as I gripped the doorpost before disappearing into the night, I stole one last look at the man. He was still staring.

A day or so later I woke, sensing I wanted something. I drew the curtains to reveal the Pōhutukawa, so close I could almost touch their leaves. Beyond them, Poplars interrupted my view of the harbour, planted by a generation who valued their beauty above the now much lauded sea view. I pulled on jodhpurs and a tee and tied back my hair, feeling purposeful, though I couldn't name the purpose, but enjoying the excitement of the unknown bubbling away.

In the kitchen, Mum was shuttling between the sink and the oven, her jandals snapping at her heels. She seemed surprised I was up, yet ever the morning person was quick with a cheerful greeting and general update.

"There isn't much movement in town," she said. "Everyone must have left last night or early this morning." She was referring to the people from the tangi (Māori funeral rite) we'd attended over the previous few days. The grounds of our schoolhouse overlooked the marae (meeting grounds), providing a prime view of the comings and goings.

"I'm going for a ride," I said. She might have preferred I have breakfast, but didn't say so, leaving me to make my own decisions as she often did.

I pulled on boots, grabbed a halter and, after collecting my pony from the paddock, tied him to the fence at the top of the drive. From there, I had a good view of the village with its pockets of houses dotting the road that snaked along the water's edge. Tea-tree blanketed hills flanked one side of the harbour, with gleaming slopes of silica sand on the other, and I could just make out the whitewash at the entrance to the harbour and hear the crash of the waves breaking on the bar.

Mum had been right; everything was quiet down at the marae. There was one car parked on the grounds, but nobody was to be seen. All the out-of-towners who'd swelled the village numbers for the tangi would now take the long, winding road home. It was an hour's drive to the first small settlement and another on to the first town.

The driveway to the school wound up through the horse paddock, cars and buses coming and going via the cattle stops at each end. The paddock's original purpose had been grazing for horses when pupils rode to school, but now none of them did that. The stark white of the concrete drive stood in direct contrast to the rest of the village where driveways were clay and the road gravel.

The girth buckles jangled as I saddled Cloudy, and metal clunked as he chewed on the bit. I put my arm around his neck, leaned into his mane, and drew a deep breath. He responded by swishing his tail lazily across his white flanks. I gathered the reins, pushed my foot into the stirrup, and swung my leg over his back. The leather creaked as I settled in the saddle and Cloudy snatched at the bit, keen to get going. We turned to head down the steep hill, my hips jarring from side to side with the pronounced movement of his hindquarters. My legs stretched as I settled in, spine undulating, vertebrae jostling for position.

Once out the gate, we passed the marae, all white-painted-wood-and-red-trim and the pensioner flats where several of the local kuia (a Māori female elder or elderly woman) lived. This was a direction I didn't normally ride as the road was short and needed a few off-road excursions to give Cloudy a good enough work out; a steep clay track up to the cemetery, or a good gallop along the beach, but I did neither.

The air was heavy, clinging to my skin, laden with moisture and motionless. I was reluctant to push Cloudy out of a walk as I could feel a barrier, a sense that the sound of trotting hooves on the gravel might rouse something best left alone. We passed the occasional stretch of grass giving way to lone tea-tree bushes, and the shadows of old 'triffid' like pines. Below the road were several homes, some only shacks or old caravans, all with curtains closed and dogs asleep on the grass outside. The canines raised their heads briefly, then slapped them down as soon as they'd established, I was friend, not foe. Past the houses to the left I could see the sea, tide out, the clay-like sand wet and exposed.

The unnamed purpose I'd begun the day with sought my attention, stirring something in my belly. It played at the edge of my mind, teasing, gently at first, before becoming insistent, pushing me past my reluctance to disturb the stillness. I pressed Cloudy into a trot, and he shot forward like he'd sensed my change in intention, and as we came up on a stretch of grass, with newfound confidence,

I pushed him into a canter. He didn't need any encouragement, bounding forward, pulling for his head, the Lipizzaner like crest of his neck rising in front of me like that of a rocking horse. The wind roared through the harness of my hard hat as Cloudy stretched out beneath me, hooves pounding the earth.

When the grass ended, we slowed to a trot and rejoined the road, the clatter of iron shoes shattering the stillness, a satisfying announcement of our presence. And now the rush was over, I let the reins loose and Cloudy stretched his neck. We were coming up fast on fences either side of the road and in front of us a couple of houses reared into view.

It was becoming obvious as we clattered along, me rising to the trot, the picture of a very correct English riding style and Cloudy with ears pricked, attentive to the fresh scenery, that we'd reached our destination. We were near the end of the road and as I pulled Cloudy up, halting in front of a gate, only then did I allow myself to admit I knew where I'd been heading. Of course, this was where the man from the marae lived.

Falling

When he said "lady with a pen", I knew it was God talking to me. I looked up from my notepad and met the eyes of the prophet. He was saying the words, but I knew they were from God, tagged by Him to draw my attention. I enjoy wielding a pen, am comfortable with one in my hand not because I'm some sort of literary genius, but I like to be organised and keep hold of the details by writing them down. And I journal a lot, penning my thoughts into red, 2B5 exercise books. Those thoughts once included a back and forth about the pen, so not only was I aware God knew how important it was to me, He knew I knew He knew.

My journal is the proving ground, the act of writing my musings a test, like someone is speaking them and I get to judge. I see them reflected off the page, and we converse, me and the pen. It's not art, it's counsel. I work at transparency, honest to a fault, always hoping mine are the only eyes that see the words in the raw. They're personal to me and God. I say things I'd feel safer keeping to myself, but that's not His plan. I've known for years He wanted me to write something from my journals, but I've kept that thought separate, so as not to write with my guard up.

The prophet went on.

"Tell your story. Tell people what you've coped with and carried, what you've worked through and what you've walked through."

It's unsurprising that God would say this, as I've examined my life, not for the purpose of telling my story but to find what set me on the path I've walked. Because if sin's graded, mine's right up there, apparently the worst of sins, something not to be spoken about. Yet God talks about it all the way through the Old Testament, using it as a metaphor for the Israelites' relationship with Him. Jesus didn't baulk at it either, befriending prostitutes and telling the woman caught in it to "go, and sin no more" (New American Standard Bible, 1971/2000, John 8:11). A few months ago a friend of mine rang distressed, having discovered a friend of hers had been caught in adultery with the pastor, past tense though. Yet it wasn't the adultery that upset her, it was the fact that in all the years they'd known each other, her friend had never confided in her. It didn't surprise me because as I said, nobody talks about it. But God wants me to.

※

2006

My first meeting with Paul didn't stand out for the reasons you'd think. When I walked into his classroom, like any teacher, he was busy talking with a group of students. He made his excuses and came over. Yet as we exchanged pleasantries, a look of consternation flitted across his face, suggesting something about me was a surprise.

"You've started on a good night. We're having a test," he said, not realizing he'd hit right at the heart of my fear. I'd battled with Billy, family friend and my husband's employer, who'd suggested I join him in taking the class.

"You can handle it," he'd said. "You won't be the only one who hasn't studied theology before."

8

Paul's eyes were sparkling, clearly enjoying my discomfort at the thought of the test.

"Have a go at it," he said, in no doubt, it seemed, that I'd put up a good showing.

I'd inherited my distaste for university level study in part from my mother, who'd vigorously warned me and my brother off, perhaps an unusual stance for a teacher to take. But business training had impacted as well, promoting in classic Southern drawl, "it don't matter how much education you've got, too much or too little, we can help you overcome it." Mostly, though, my reticence was because I didn't want to look stupid.

Paul's class had been meeting for a couple of weeks, which meant I was playing catch up. There were around twenty students, so it was going to be hard to hide what I was fast discovering. I was out of my depth. That aside, I enjoyed watching Paul interact with the students, his hunger to teach flowing out of him, and when someone in the class tried to trip him up, perhaps to impress, his response honoured them whilst successfully engaging with their position. He was relaxed, not concerned if people questioned his teaching, just wanting the truth and happy for the class to search it out together.

As the lesson progressed, it became clear why Paul had a reputation as one of the best bible teachers in New Zealand. He told us we need to hear the Lord as a child, to hear Him speak to us even through a child, and Paul did indeed create that environment. There were no dumb questions, and rather than presenting himself as the fount of all knowledge, he facilitated exchanges between class members. He was never at a loss, always able to quote scripture to make his point, and if someone quoted the bible, he knew the book, chapter, and verse. His depth of knowledge was inspiring, the way he built a case for each point with scripture pulled from many areas of the bible. It was the most intense teaching I'd ever experienced. I trained my eyes on him, listening intently, and by the end of the lesson I felt sated, like I'd eaten a richly satisfying meal.

During the weeks that followed, he started a series of seminars at the church he led. Of course, given my delight with his weekly bible classes, I went along. Again, the standard of teaching was high. I hung on every word, and during the lunch break chatted with him at the back of the room. He was responsive, giving the impression I was worthy of his attention, though a short time into our conversation he drew a sharp breath, checked his watch, and abruptly excused himself, saying it was time to get back to the teaching. I watched him walk away, thinking how very nice he was, and as I took my seat, I noticed I was feeling sated again. He called everyone back, and while they filtered into the auditorium, I wondered whether it was possible that someone could be too nice.

That night I stole out of bed at one or two in the morning, ducked into my son's room to check on him before heading downstairs, making a cup of tea, and slipping into the office. I sat and stared at the empty computer, taking the occasional sip of tea, and replaying the tapes in my head, the ones where during the previous day and at other times, Paul had singled me out for attention. I played the tapes over and over.

While I'd been attending the weekly bible classes, the home-based church group we'd been a part of for several years began fellowshipping at Paul's church. I was attending the service for the third time as part of the congregation. There were people posted at the door greeting all comers, others were busy in the kitchen, and multiple groups dotted around chatting. Some were sitting quietly, others laughing raucously about some All Blacks or

Black Caps result, and it was all accompanied by the cacophony of the worship team warming up in the background.

The building was a converted warehouse large enough to house a full-sized gymnasium where the kids could play safely in any weather, and a multitude of other rooms suitable for use as offices or for small group meetings. There was also rental space creating a welcome additional income, and just inside the front door was a café, where I was standing chatting when Paul's wife Marie spotted me as she tore through the entrance. She veered off track to join my conversation.

"Hey," she said, with eyes only for me, "we need to work together to integrate your group into the church whanau (family). We should get together to chat about it." I hadn't been a leader in our home church, yet she seemed to want me to help bridge the gap between our group and the church.

The following Sunday, Marie again found me in the café, startling my co-conversationalist with her vigorous interruption.

"Oh, Simone," she said, "we got your email about helping with the church admin. Thanks for that."

It wasn't the reaction I'd been expecting. At Paul's theology class earlier in the week, I'd told him I loved paperwork, something he'd been unable to fathom, and during a previous Sunday message I'd taken note when he'd mentioned the church ran on volunteers. Sometime later, a scripture had come to my attention about our gifts being for use in the kingdom, so, in the email Marie was referring to, I'd offered to help because the church had recently lost admin staff.

"You know, Paul wasn't aiming at your group when he said the church ran on volunteers," she said.

"I didn't think he was, just what he said stood out to me."

"It's just your offer seems driven, that's all," she said, and walked off.

It was her use of the word 'driven' that got me. For some time, the space she'd vacated held my attention.

The Warning

In my family, 'knowing' is a thing, 'seeing' and 'feeling' too. My grandmother was fey, that's what everyone said. She claimed to know about things before they happened. She claimed other things too. I can remember her telling the story of having felt my dead grandfather bang on the back of her seat in the car. She'd looked behind, but there'd been no one there. And my mother has always spoken of similar things, claiming once she'd been aware of an impending accident when I'd been driving to Auckland and she'd quickly prayed. We realised later her prayer had come at the same time I'd driven around a tight corner to find a truck on my side of the road. I'd only just squeezed the car between him and the clay wall.

I realise now I've always just accepted it as true; them being fey, really with no evidence or even many stories to back it up. Possibly the reason I've done so is that I have my own stories of supernatural occurrences.

Paul's next theology lesson started badly. Billy and I arrived late, which seemed to irk Paul, and then there was some back and forth over a scriptural issue, Billy on one side and Paul and the rest of the class on the other. It was all well above my head. Billy was obviously upset and as soon as the class ended, he wanted to leave. Because

I'd travelled with him, I had to go too, which was disappointing as I could see the other students hanging around to talk some more over a coffee.

Billy and I were about to drive off when I realised I'd forgotten to ask Paul a question about the assignment he'd set for the class.

"I'll just email him later," I said.

"No," said Billy, "he's right there at the door. Run and ask."

It was dark, so Paul was locking up. He saw me coming and opened the door just wide enough for us to talk, but left no room for me to enter. I could see the others standing in the light behind him talking and laughing, and as I spoke, I sensed them wanting me to hurry so Paul could get back to their conversation. Paul must have felt it too because he answered my question hurriedly, glancing over his shoulder a couple of times and giving me no encouragement to seek further clarification, but somehow, I remained rooted in place. Even though I knew Paul wanted me to go, I couldn't.

There was a pause, this quiet moment during which he must've asked himself why I wasn't leaving, and I felt the expectation, but I couldn't move. It seemed what was happening was straddling two realms, with something traversing the barrier between them. I was looking at Paul but seeing a picture of a rustic dungeon gate between us, like the gate of The Colosseum in the movie *Gladiator*. It even had spikes on the end of the vertical bars. I saw the gate drop, and I felt, as well as heard, the resounding clang and boom as the weight of it crashed into the ground.

It took a moment for me to break off my gaze, I'd been so caught up in the vision. Paul was looking at me like he thought I was acting strangely. I took a step back from the door, my eyes still locked on him, then I turned and walked away. I don't even know if I said goodbye. I walked slowly, not wanting to get back to the car or Billy too soon, just needing a little time to consider what I'd just seen, but I felt rather than intellectually understood what the gate meant. It was God warning me off, telling me, "Don't touch My anointed."

The warning frightened me, and other situations of concern arose, adding to my fears. I needed to talk to my mentor Beth, but considering I hadn't contacted her earlier when I'd first noticed the feelings of satiety in relation to Paul, it was going to look like I'd been hiding things.

My husband, Steve, had added to the 'concerning situations' tally, coming home full of news after meeting Paul for the first time at work.

"You must've made quite an impact on him," he said. "He's really impressed with you, made quite a point of telling me, 'There's just something about Simone, isn't there?'"

Since then, I'd been feeding my pride on that little statement, so I knew it was time to ring Beth.

"I've slipped a little with Paul," I said. There was silence at the other end of the line, so I continued, thinking maybe I hadn't made myself clear. "I think he's wary of me now."

Front of mind was a gathering at Billy and his wife Pauline's home, a barbeque, our group's first social event with the church since we'd formally joined. I hadn't realised then, but later—a whole two weeks later—it'd finally occurred to me what I'd been up to that night.

I'd been helping with the dishes and there'd been a group of people, including Paul, chatting in the kitchen. I'd needed to put some crockery away beside them and, bending low, had moved through the group, dropping to my haunches to reach the back of the cupboard. It sounds innocent, but it wasn't. When I bent down, I glanced at him, causing him to step back. It flustered him, which to my mind suggested I was making an impression. As I'd dropped to my haunches, I'd assessed the effect I was having. My movements were sensual, designed to attract his attention, and as I reversed and stood up, I'd looked at him again. He'd smiled self-effacingly and my attitude had been, 'like a lamb to the slaughter'.

It was bad enough I hadn't realised what I was doing, but the reason for my sudden need to talk to Beth was I'd just returned from another one of Paul's seminars at the church, the last in his series of three. I'd waited all day for him to smile at me, or at least look at me in the crowd, but there'd been none of that and I'd felt its absence. The teaching had been exciting, so my feelings of disappointment confirmed I was now desperately in need of his acknowledgment. Yet it seemed he was distancing himself, which made sense of the vision I'd had of the dungeon gate coming down between us. I now believed that somehow, he'd picked up on my behaviour and suspected my heart in the relationship. So, the dungeon gate warning, plus the thought that Paul might have figured me out, was what had eventually driven me to call Beth. She finally came to life at the other end of the line.

"How come you didn't discuss this sooner?"

How like her to pick up on my lack of transparency, the one question I really didn't want to answer. Obviously, I hadn't mentioned it earlier because I didn't want to stop what I was doing; it was like food, and I was starving. When I didn't answer, she helped me out.

"Where were your needs and thoughts at? Did you think you'd worked on this problem, got it sussed, figured you could relax?"

Ah, Beth, never slow to get right to the nub of things.

"I went back to that place where I needed to be noticed, and I couldn't stop myself acting on it," I said. It was a blatant admission I'd been aware of the problem on some level and had deliberately kept it from her.

"What happened? Were you bored and wanted something to entertain yourself with?"

Ouch, I cringed. Beth was in full force. She paused for a moment, and I thought it was to gather herself, but then I realised she was calming herself down, so she didn't rip up one side of me and down the other. I heard her take a deep breath.

"This is very much a part of the pattern of how you've related to people most of your life. Look, it takes time to put up the scaffolding that will make it possible to rebuild you, to make the alterations necessary. I wonder if you took away the scaffolding too soon?"

"Yes—maybe I did, and now I'm embarrassed. I don't know how to be around him or anyone else, for that matter."

"Okay, okay," she said, pleased I think to hear me acknowledge my mistake. "Get your hope back on and go back to the basics. Go before your God and your King—he will deal with the embarrassment—and relate to Paul like he's a friend of your husband, or a colleague."

"Okay ..."

"You can build out again from there," she said.

"Yes, okay—thank you Beth."

She spent a moment checking I'd understood what I needed to do and then hung up. Which should've been the end of it, but unfortunately, there was more.

In that I thought I was being open and honest and then had discovered I'd been playing games with Paul; it opened my eyes to other things I'd been up to. It was disturbing to believe I was doing well, only to find clear evidence I wasn't, and that it had taken me so long to figure that out. It was like I'd hit my head, lost my memory and then been slow to regain it. I didn't want to embarrass myself by making the same mistake again, so I figured I had to talk with Beth about the other issue. I'd just give her a few days to get over this one.

I emailed her this time, telling her about my offer a month earlier to help with the admin at church, and that they'd just come back saying they had something for me. Paul and others had bypassed his wife Marie's concerns about me seeming 'driven', a big mistake, and wanted me to help with the admin at church every Tuesday morning during the school term. I couldn't believe the timing. It made it obvious I'd been keeping pertinent things from Beth. In the email, I asked whether she thought it was a mistake for me to spend more time at the church, but if she thought it was okay, could I hold myself accountable to her? I wasn't sure how she'd react given I'd already hidden stuff, but she emailed me the same day:

> You will need to be straight up and give me short accounts of what is going on in your thoughts and emotions ...

I can remember the relief I felt. Not because I knew Beth was going to help me, but because I knew she wouldn't stand in my way.

Church Keys

I think Anne, who ran the church office, may have been another like Paul's wife Marie, who didn't think I should work at the church. Or maybe she was testing my mettle. Anyway, whatever the reason, she started me on some particularly menial tasks. Paul's office was across the mezzanine floor from hers, and the kitchen where Anne had me sorting cutlery was in his view when he crossed between the two. He'd seen me a few times on his trips back and forth, and on one of them, he came over.

"So, you're the new admin support?" he said with a big grin, eyes sparkling.

"Yep, here to help with all that paperwork," I said, clattering the cutlery for dramatic effect. He laughed, both of us acknowledging the conversation we'd had about my love of paperwork.

"What are you doing?" he said, a slight frown flitting across his face.

"I'm sorting cutlery." His eyes widened, and he opened his mouth in mock horror. I laughed. "It's okay—I don't mind."

"Yeah, but surely there's something more important for you to be doing?"

"I think Anne is just getting to know me. It's okay."

He didn't speak for a moment, but I could tell he wanted to say more. I didn't want him to go, so I just continued sorting, not giving any sign our conversation might have finished, and eventually he went on.

"We're having a meeting soon, the admin team—you should come."

I smiled, noticing I was basking in the warmth of knowing he wanted me there.

"Not until I've finished this important business," I said, waving my hand over the piles of cutlery. He laughed and walked away, telling me they'd be meeting in the admin office in a few minutes.

I was pleased at Paul's invitation, but felt the pressure. I wasn't part of the team; it might appear all kinds of wrong to the other staff. I didn't want it to look like Paul wanted me around more than he should have. The meeting was tense with the others having strong disagreements, but at least that gave me the chance to sit back and watch. Paul tried to draw me into some discussions, but I noticed the others weren't happy about it, so I didn't contribute as fully as I could have.

The meeting went on for at least an hour and by the end, my tension levels and sensitivity to Paul and the others were off the scale. I was 'sonaring' wildly, my word for the way I'd send out signals; glances, different levels of eye contact, even the movements I made, and then I'd work out the effect they were having by reading people's reactions. And I wasn't only doing it in relation to Paul. It was an exhausting way to behave, and unfortunately, I didn't notice how much the effort was affecting my level of resolve to be near Paul and still leave him alone, as per my agreement with Beth.

After the meeting, Anne asked me to clean out an office that, over time, had turned into a junk room. The key was missing, so she told me to ask Paul for the spare. When I arrived in his doorway, he was at his desk, intently studying a book. The room looked disheveled, clearly furnished with bits of furniture cobbled together from nowhere in particular. It gave the impression the church didn't value him. I knocked, and when he saw me, his face lit up and I sucked in the attention. When I asked for the key, he handed me an enormous wad. There must have been some fifty keys on the ring. My face obviously conveyed that he had to be kidding. He laughed, and as I held them, he sorted through to find the right one.

"It's this one ... or this one," he said, pulling out two keys and looking apologetic.

I walked the one or two doors down the hall and tried the first key. I was hoping it wouldn't work, and I got what I wanted. I tried the second with the same result. Immediately I wanted to call out to Paul but thought that might appear needy, so I tried the keys again. It would've been embarrassing if he'd come to my rescue and opened the door with ease. When again they didn't work, I walked back to his office and, guessing I'd been unsuccessful, he led the way back to the door, leaving room for me to pass in front of him and telling me to try again. I was a bit surprised. I thought he'd just take the keys and try the door.

Now, there are times when the rhythm of life slows down, in much the same way a metronome alters its pace as you move the weight up the bar. This was one of those times. I should have known to take care, should have felt the change, but to my shame, I reveled in the experience, desperately trying to draw it out. I could feel something coming, an affirmation that I had indeed made an impression on Paul, and I wanted to garner all I could out of whatever happened.

As I was trying the first key, my skin tightened, and I liked it, the way the heightened sensitivity made me feel. I paid attention to it and more than that; I danced with it, ramping up the significance of the moment by foisting all my attention on what I imagined was going on between us. He was behind me, three, probably four feet. I was keenly aware of him as I put the second key in the lock and turned it, dipping my head and looking up at him as I did. I couldn't be sure if he was looking at me, or more at what I was doing, but he had a wry smile on his face which I couldn't gauge the meaning of. I felt like a performer on stage, being watched and assessed, yet unable to discern the result of the assessment, which was an unusual circumstance for me, as my 'sonaring' had honed my skills in that area.

I should have heeded the metronomic slow down, a blatant warning, and adjusted my attitude, but I kept on engaging with the emotion. I wanted him to move in behind me, place his arms over and around my arm and hand, and firmly help me turn the key. I wanted him to take charge, and I needed to believe I'd caused him to do so.

But as suddenly as the rhythm had slowed, it sped up again. Paul didn't move closer to me and, as if the gears of life suddenly caught, the moment stuttered. Paul laughed, a reaction so out of place it jerked my thinking back to the key in the lock. I rocked it from side to side. It caught, and I heard the click of the bolt moving. I pushed open the door and walked into the room.

You Got Any Balls?

My story really began at the gate of the man from the marae. Sitting there on Cloudy waiting for signs of life to appear from the house, I'd felt embarrassed. Up till then, collecting my pony from the paddock, saddling him and throughout the ride, I hadn't been conscious of my intentions, but the moment I felt embarrassment, that pointed to awareness. I'd waited expectantly and, even though the doors and windows of the house had been closed, I'd still called out a couple of times. Just as I turned to leave, the man's cousin appeared, her brow creased, stance questioning my presence. I had no answer, no legitimate reason to be there, so I spluttered an excuse, asking after the man, and when she told me he wasn't home, I turned tail and left.

I think about the girl I was that day; wonder what connection the man had made the night or two before when he'd stared at me. I felt I'd mesmerised him, that there was something so transfixing about me it had captured him. I could trace my previous experience of that feeling to an after-show party of *Bluebeard* that my mother had taken me to when I was eight or nine years old. She'd been a musician in the orchestra. A friend of hers had taken a special interest in me, capturing my attention by kindly showing me a pianola behind the stage. Then amid the party revelers he'd danced with me, flattering me with his undivided attention. It pleased me to think I'd impacted him, that there was something attractive about me. But later, in the car on the way home, my mother unceremoniously disavowed me of that opinion, crassly stating in front of my father and brother too, that the man's attentiveness had been because of his interest in her.

Early '80s

It wasn't long after my encounter with the man on the marae that my family shifted, and as soon as we arrived in the small farming community in a picturesque valley several hours out of Auckland, Joylene and I found each other. She lived a couple of hundred metres down the road, was only a year younger, and shared my interest in all things equine.

On a ride around the top of the valley one afternoon, she was singing a Hot Chocolate single, one of her favourites, and a top ten track.

"It started with a kiss ... in the backroom of the cowshed ... how could I resist ... the aroma of the cow-shit ..."

I turned in the saddle to look at her. "Eh? What are you on about?" Then it hit me, and I gasped. "You kissed him?" She kicked her mare and jogged up beside me, a cheeky grin on her face.

"He kissed me," she said, tipping her head up to emphasise her point, causing her ill-fitting hard hat to drop over her eyes, making what should have been a romantic statement seem slightly humorous. "Yep," she said guessing the question I was too dumbstruck to ask, "in the pit during milking. While we were waiting for a row to finish." She said it like she'd won something.

"How'd he get on to that, then?" I couldn't imagine a man of his age, a farmer, bothering with a thirteen-year-old girl, but it made sense of her interest in helping him on his farm.

24

Cloudy jogged beneath me and I instinctively pulled on the reins.

"We'd just sprayed the cows ..." she was talking about the lanolin which prevents cow's teats from cracking, "we were standing down the end of the pit and he was just looking at me ... acting strange, and then he just leaned in ... and kissed me!" She was triumphant again.

I heard a car coming, so I pushed Cloudy on, reverting to single file. It was one of the locals in his Ute, dust etched into its paintwork from years of traversing metal roads. I smiled and waved, and he nonchalantly lifted a hand as his vehicle rolled past.

"Has he done anything like that before?" I said, pulling Cloudy up so Joylene could ride alongside again.

"Maybe."

I looked at her hard, knowing she wouldn't be able to resist telling me more, and she looked away, then back, laughing.

"We've played around a bit ..."

I gave her the eye again.

"... in the hay barn ... y'know."

"No—I don't know!"

"Just mucking around really ... chasing each other ... throwing hay—little bit of touching." She pushed her glasses up the bridge of her nose with the back of her hand.

"Ooh, touching ... where?"

"Not there!" she said, our laughter causing our ponies to jog.

"How old is he?"

"Twenty-four," she said. "Already share milking with his dad."

I needed some time to digest that little snippet of information. How had she attracted a man like that?

"You wanna go?" I said, indicating a stretch of grass where we often cantered. I was finding it difficult to maintain eye contact, battling my disbelief at her being attractive enough to have gained this man's attention. She pushed her mare into a trot and Cloudy lurched forward, straight into a canter, chasing her down. He pulled hard, wanting his head so he could get past the mare. I let him go. It was just easier to give him what he wanted. When we pulled up again, Cloudy's shoes clattered on the metal road and Joylene's unshod mare stumbled, causing her to jerk forward then slap back in the saddle.

"Ouch ... that hurt," she said, pulling at the seat of her jeans.

I laughed at her as we settled back into our side-by-side walk.

"I'm gonna help Mike again tomorrow," she said, glancing about to make sure nobody was around since we were coming up on houses at more regular intervals. "I just have to talk my mum into letting me go."

I didn't think she'd get her wish; her parents were strict.

"Well, behave yourself—don't do anything I wouldn't do ..."

She giggled, reveling in the attention, as well she should. She'd scored a real coup.

I met Joylene's Mike at the old school building turned community hall that stood between our houses. We'd heard his motorbike pull up at the gate and were walking across the tennis courts just as he was leaving the pool enclosure. When he saw us, he altered course.

"G'day!" he said, all 'hail-fellow-well-met.'

"Hi" I said.

Joylene strode towards him, springing off her toes, thighs flaring below her jean shorts like succulent drumsticks. It wasn't unpleasant, just sizeable, and I admired her lack of self-consciousness. I was relatively slim, but not comfortable wearing clothes like that.

"Hey" she said, tilting her chin up and running her hands through her hair.

"What are you two up to?" he said.

I liked how he included me. I hadn't met him before, but I knew who he was. Every time we left the valley, we had to drive through his farm, so I'd seen him many times. He was always in his green overalls or blue Stubbies shorts, following his herd of Jerseys as they crossed the road into the yards, one of his black 'n' tans sitting on his bike's fuel tank, the other on the seat behind. If the cows were all over the road, he'd speak one or two words and his dogs would leap off the bike like little heat-seeking missiles, careering up behind the cows, snapping at their heels. He was looking at us searchingly now. I didn't know what to say, but Joylene knew him. I figured it was her job to attend to the conversation.

"We're just hanging around," she said.

"Just hanging around, eh?" he said. I found it odd he repeated what she'd just said, word for word. "Good day for a game of tennis, isn't it?"

"You wanna game then?" Joylene said.

"Could do," he said, looking from her to me. I wondered, was he just including me with the look, or was it a personal invitation?

"We probably wanna get a game in before it gets too hot," I said, pleased I could add something, and to answer Mike's possible personal invitation.

"You played much?" he said.

"A little."

"It's getting hot out here," Joylene said, walking under the tree where Mike was. I thought it was obvious what she was up to, but I followed anyway and sat beside her on the bank. Mike dropped to his haunches and pulled at some grass.

Joylene suddenly shoved me in the side.

"What the heck ..." I said, trying to regain my composure, wanting to remain cool. She looked at me, then pointedly at Mike and back at me, raising her eyebrows. Oh wow, he wasn't wearing any underwear and when he'd squatted his shorts had ridden up giving us a bird's-eye view. She looked at me and we giggled. Mike didn't seem to notice and was looking down, feigning interest in the grass.

"I'll go get my racquet then, shall I?" he said. We were still sniggering, and he looked up, slightly puzzled.

"You got any balls?" Joylene asked, and then she dissolved. I felt embarrassed for him, and busied myself standing up, brushing down my pants. Joylene's sisters were coming down the road, which didn't bode well. They'd hang around being annoying or have a message from her Mum, that she needed to do some chore or other.

"Ya' sisters are coming," I said. She looked up, a disgruntled expression replacing the laughter.

"What d'ya want?" she yelled, standing up. Her sister Tabitha went to say something, but Joylene's attitude and Mike's presence seemed to silence her. It was the younger one that spoke.

"Mum wants you to come home."

Joylene looked at me long-sufferingly and turned. "I'll come back as soon as I can ... I'll bring my racquet," she said over her shoulder, stomping across the court with her sisters in tow.

I looked at Mike. Fortunately, when the girls had arrived, he'd stood up.

"I'll give you a lift home," he said, correctly assuming that would be okay with me. I followed him to his motorbike, noticing his muscly legs looked stick person like, incongruous between his short shorts and sizeable gumboots. He had a long stride, and I had to jog to keep up. When he got to his bike, he kicked the stand up and swung his leg over the saddle.

"Jump on," he said, turning to face forward. I sidled up to the bike. "Put your hand here," he said, tapping his shoulder, "and just step over."

I was very aware of how close I was to him, the smell of spoilt milk and cow crap emanating from his clothes. As he stood to kick start the bike, I leant back and held onto the tray. As soon as his backside hit the seat the bike moved off and he drove the few hundred metres to my house. He went past and u-turned, pulling up in front of our fence, leaving the engine running. I quickly, if somewhat inelegantly, pulled my leg back over the bike. As he moved off, he looked past me and waved at Mum standing at the kitchen window.

"See you soon," he said, gunning the engine and roaring up the gears as he pulled away.

It turned out he was a good tennis player. I whipped around the court, getting the occasional shot over on him, but Joylene stumbled around with her racquet flailing, making me look good by comparison. That game was the first of many as we three began spending evenings and weekends working on his farm and having fun relaxing together afterwards, playing tennis, table tennis, going out on the boat, even one disastrous attempt at water skiing. I had never had so much fun.

During the school holidays, on a day when neither Joylene nor Mike were around, I went looking for dad to ask him for a game of tennis. He'd been a top player in his day with a lethal serve, something he could still achieve, especially since he had a lot more weight to put behind it now. Yet despite his large frame, within the family he always seemed to blend into the background, quietly off doing his own thing; in the garage tinkering with the car, wrestling with a woodworking project, or in the darkroom developing prints. In more reflective moments, he'd be sitting in the lounge puffing on a fat cigar, classical music on the turntable, and a leg draped over the arm of the chair.

I spotted him arriving home, probably from the local garage where in later years I learned from mum he'd often gone to get his secret stash of chocolate. He hauled himself out of his little Daihatsu Charade like he was levering open a tin can, slammed the door, and as he headed up the path, I dogged his steps, racquet in hand. He was on a mission, barely seeming to register I was behind him.

"Dad, ya wanna game of tennis?"

"No, I'm busy," he said, walking into the house, leaving me stopped dead in his wake.

Perhaps if he'd said, "maybe later," or "sorry, I'm busy" it might have softened his delivery, but because he'd just powered on as if I were an irritant, using his size to push me away, it'd really hurt. Unfortunately, the way I read it was 'don't touch me', and many years later I deduced I'd extrapolated his irritation and lack of desire to spend time with me, to mean 'you're ugly'. For me to have asked him to play means there must have been times when he did, but fairly or unfairly, at that point I gave up expecting anything other than what he was comfortable giving.

I'd always hoped for more, seen him as my protector in a slightly removed sense; his size and strength a threat causing others to be wary of harming me. There'd been the time three boys had chased me down the beach, yet, when they'd caught up, hadn't harmed me, just circled threateningly. My dad had been their teacher and for most of my life, I believed they hadn't touched me because of the physical threat he posed and his position of authority over them. I'd also been told my dad was proud of me, though I hadn't felt it. He'd come to my horse events regularly for a time, to photograph everyone, not just me, and there were moments where he congratulated me on some of my achievements. But I'd never felt the delight, the obvious pleasure I'd seen other men express towards their daughters.

So, though I didn't know who I thought I was addressing as I stood in his wake at our back door that day, the many years of not feeling his love closed in and I vowed, 'Dad, I'll never ask you to do anything with me again.' I turned on the spot, went back down the path and out the gate, leaving the clunk of the latch to echo through my life.

Lucky, but Ute-less

At some point, our farming threesome became two. In the beginning, every school morning after the bus had picked me up, its next stop would be Joylene's gate. Her habit had been to climb up the steps, look down to the end of the bus, smile and head to the back to sit with the group. Then, out of the blue, things changed. She'd get on the bus, spin round at the top step, and plonk herself in the nearest seat. I didn't think about the fact that she'd stopped turning up at Mike's as well, but it became clear from her behaviour on the bus that now it was just him and me. Since I had him to myself, I asked why he'd kissed her, and he told me it was because she'd wanted him to.

In June, on my fifteenth birthday, Mike came around with a huge box and a mischievous grin. I opened the box only to find another box, and inside that scrunched up newspaper and a round object wrapped in birthday paper. I didn't know what it could be. Mike was watching, eyes glittering, and I looked to him for a hint, but he was giving nothing away. I opened the birthday paper and found a tyre, about the size of one you'd put on a motor mower. Mike laughed, enjoying my confusion.

"Shake it," he said.

There was a rattle, and inside the arch of the tyre I found a blue velvet box. As I flipped it open, I noticed Mike shifting his weight from side to side.

"Wow, thanks," I said.

It contained a delicate gold necklace with a sapphire pendant which he wanted to put on me, but I told him I could do it and hurried to the mirror in the hall.

I don't remember when he first kissed me or when we first had sex, though both certainly happened, and well before the gift of the necklace. What I do remember is how the whole situation got me down. There was the repetitive question, "are we gonna make it?", during which I'd have to appease him, and then there was the doomed overnight trip to the field days in Hamilton, where a little horseplay ended in Mike suffering a sharp knee to the nether regions. Logically, I hadn't been in any danger, but emotionally, my instinctive reaction suggested I wasn't so sure.

The necklace, and Mike's insistence I keep telling him our relationship was going to last, both stated something I wasn't freely assenting to. I overrode the lead feeling in my stomach, told him the necklace was pretty, and that, yes, we were gonna make it. All the while, underneath my sense of success at having hooked the wealthy older man, someone who my parents seemed to so strongly approve of, I felt I was being purchased. There was power in my position, but I was coming to understand, that power didn't equal freedom.

"You're a lucky girl," my mum said, at the gift of the necklace. She seemed pleased. Dad was smiling, but he made no comment and then disappeared. I knew Mum had always wanted to marry a farmer, that she saw farming as the good life, so apparently, I'd struck gold early. It made me terrified of throwing it all away, so the relationship continued, and as soon as I got my University Entrance, I left school to work full time on Mike's farm.

When we'd been together for two years, I became reticent to spend time with him, and he noticed. One day, he deliberately arrived at the house when Mum and Dad had gone out. Just outside our front door we had a picnic table, solid, my dad had made it, and we were sitting on the tabletop, backs to each other, with our feet on the seats. Mike wanted us to go to bed together, and though I had my back to him, I could tell he'd twisted around to look at me. He was busy letting me know how long it'd been since we'd slept together, as if he thought that would be encouraging.

"I don't want to," I said, half turning his way. He laced his hands through his hair and rubbed back and forth roughly, leaving it standing on end. It was classic Rumpelstiltskin, something he often did when frustrated with the cows, and now with his hair at crazy angles he looked unstable. However, his dramatics didn't have the effect he wanted, so he changed tack.

"Shall we have a cup of tea then?"

Maybe he'd given up, but it could also mean he thought if we were inside, it would be easier to get me to oblige.

"I don't feel like a tea."

"What are we gonna do then?" he said, face red, the veins on his forehead distended.

I looked at my hands. "I don't wanna do anything." I thought if I just stayed there responding only if I had to, there'd be nothing he could do; eventually he'd have to leave.

I could hear a car coming down the road, going quick, the thwap as it ran along the one lane bridge, the short period of wheels on metal again, and the whirr as the car hit the tar seal outside the community hall. The vehicle slowed and turned into the driveway opposite the school. Though Mike was quiet, he was still communicating. I was keeping busy by justifying my position to myself. I didn't need his money; I didn't need to be working for him. I'd find something else.

It seemed interminable, but eventually he got up. He had to walk past me to get to the gate and he glared, stuffed his hands in the pockets of his overalls and stalked down the path. At the gate, he turned to throw me an accusatory look, which I held, refusing to cower. He slammed the gate behind him, the latch clanging violently, and the whole fence rocked. He grabbed his bike, revving the engine wildly, instantly creating a skid mark as he took off. He roared violently up the gears as he headed down the road.

Relief coursed through me, but it didn't last long. I didn't know where things stood, how I would be next time I saw him, how he would be, and how I was going to transport my horses without his ute to pull my float.

I got off the picnic table and walked inside, wandering through the house into the kitchen. It was quiet. I wondered what time Mum and Dad would be back. The sun was streaming in the kitchen window, blinding as it hit the glass on top of the kitchen table. I opened the fridge, grabbed the butter and vegemite, and put on the jug for a cup of tea.

"Let's Dance"

It's hard thinking back to this time in my life. From this distance I feel fear, and sorry for my younger self. There was nothing solid I could let my weight down on. I was completely alone in the position I'd put myself. My friends were just as stupid as I was, and I felt no security with my parents, didn't trust them with any of my emotions, and didn't see them as having any wisdom in the issues I was dealing with. I can point to a couple of incidents which must have informed my thinking, the first after a party I'd attended where none of the young men had shown any interest in me. I was being taught by correspondence, but really spending my days watching soaps. I was very lonely and the young men overlooking me had been crushing. In bed that night, after the party, I started howling, completely distraught, the rejection and loneliness coinciding. My mother had come running because of the noise I was making, but she hadn't seemed capable of comforting me.

Similarly, within a year of that night, my cat, which I'd had since I was five years old, ran out on the road and under a car. I'd gone into my parent's room crying, again distraught, wherein my mother had told me I'd be alright and sent me away to deal with my emotions on my own.

Mid to late '80s

The disquiet around my relationship with Mike tainted my whole life. Up till then, I'd been working on his farm seven days a week with one weekend off a month. Every day I'd been up at 4am to help milk the cows, so we'd have finished the last row when the tanker arrived at 7am. On weekdays, after a full breakfast made by Mike's mum, we'd done the general work around the farm. The type of work had depended on the season, a lot of hay in the summer, then during calving, it had centered on the animals. At other times there'd been fencing, fertilising, and maintenance work. After milking in the afternoons, on weekends, Mike had been having dinner at our place, and weekdays, he'd had dinner at his parent's. Either way, he'd been spending most nights at our place, ostensibly on the spare bed in my room.

Into the midst of our now strained situation strolled a friend of Mike's. I'd been off work sick the day Joey, who lived down the road, came over to have a drink with my dad. It was probably my back I was home sick with. I'd had Valium prescribed for the pain, but I was using the drug to check out of my situation with Mike. When his friend Joey wandered into our house that evening, it was like the out from my situation had just walked in.

I heard Joey talking with dad. Through Mike, I'd spent a bit of time with him, and I liked him. He was fun. I loved his cockney accent and the smooth timbre of his voice. It was rich, like a shot of adrenalin, and it drew me out of my room into the kitchen where he was sitting with a glass of wine in front of him, his back to the window. His eyes took me in, invigorating me, as if a new substance was flowing through my veins.

"'Allo," he said with a smile, the laughing cadence of his voice colliding with my fragile state of mind.

"Hi" I said. His eyes sucked the breath out of me, and I turned away to hide the impact. I felt sure he'd seen my reaction and been aware of his effect. I grabbed a cup and busied myself spooning coffee and sugar into it. Dad tried to carry on the conversation they'd been having, but it sounded disjointed now.

I needed the milk and Joey was beside the fridge, so I gathered myself to turn into the full force of his gaze. Being prepared didn't prevent the breath being knocked out of me again. I had to coach myself, keep my eyes on the fridge, get the milk. He smiled as I came close, and the aroma of his cologne wafted towards me. I just wanted to saturate myself in it.

I finished making my coffee and left the room, turning on the television in the lounge and flopping onto the couch. I wasn't paying any attention to what was on tv, but listening to the conversation in the kitchen. Joey stayed for a long time; I think way longer than dad would have liked, and I waited in the lounge, unable to trust myself to go back in the kitchen. With the television unable to hold my interest, I turned on some music.

Suddenly the door opened, and Joey slipped in, drink in hand, making a beeline for the stereo. I think dad had gone to the toilet. I'd been playing music that made me feel good, hoping I'd attract Joey's attention, but now he was in the room, I didn't know how to be around him.

I needn't have worried; he handled the situation. He examined the album cover; it was probably The Cars. I walked over, pretending interest in what he was looking at, and he turned to me. He was taller, around six feet, so he was looking down. He had a distinctive nose, with very little angular definition from the forehead which I'd seen in other people from the UK. He smiled, like it seemed he always was, and after looking as if he were considering his options, he held out his hand.

"Let's dance," he said. I put my hand in his and he pulled me close. I'd danced with him at socials and parties, but it was the first time we'd been in a room alone and I wasn't ready for the impact the seclusion contributed. He wrapped his arms around me, and I melted into his fabulous chest. I think he liked that physically and emotionally he had me in the palm of his hand. We undulated to the music, his hands roaming up and down my back.

I lost all sense of time and propriety, adrift in some world where all that mattered was the pleasure of being wrapped in his embrace. He drew back slightly, looked down, and lifted my chin. It felt like a scene from a movie as he kissed me, so lost in the moment I didn't think about his wife and child at home, just down the road. Nor did I heed the thought that my mother or father could walk in at any moment.

Eventually dad came back but seemed unsure of how to handle the situation, speaking to us like we were both young people, telling me it was time I went to bed. Joey laughed, seemingly unperturbed by being treated like a teenager. He picked up his glass and left the room, chuckling to himself.

I switched off the music and, as my dad saw Joey out, dived across the hall into my bedroom to avoid my dad's return journey. I was keen to be left alone to bathe in the afterglow of what had just happened.

Shadow Play

Eventually, I built up the courage to tell Mike I didn't want to see him anymore. I did it in the kitchen at home.

"So that's it then, is it?" he said, his eyes dark, the veins in his neck distended.

"Yes." I slammed my mouth shut on the word, like I was taking back something I'd lost. He stormed past me, heading for the door.

"Mike! Don't go," Mum said, appearing from the hallway. He didn't break stride but tore open the door, swinging round, steely eyed, to deliver one last reprimand. Mum rushed after him, watching as he disappeared into the night.

I moved on, taking up the offer of a job from Joey. He had a one-person operation milking a hundred cows. He'd pay me the same wage Mike did, but I only had to milk morning and night, which left the middle of the day free to work my horses. Joey said we'd do the first milking together so he could teach me how his machinery worked and acquaint me with his methods.

"Just get yourself down to the shed when you see the cows coming in," he said.

When I arrived, he was professional, and were it not lodged in my memory, I could easily have thought I'd imagined the kiss in our lounge.

His milking shed was newer and a lot smaller than Mikes. It was like playing at farming in comparison. Joey showed me his routine to prepare the machines, and we got started. I was acutely aware of his every move, as he zig-zagged across the pit, switching the cups from the cows on one side to the other. His energy level was high, making him fun to work with, his bright orange overalls correctly suggesting a playful spirit. In between rows, while we waited for the cows to milk out, we chatted about the ones that might misbehave and those with other issues I needed to be aware of. He was the consummate boss, and I relaxed into the routine, comfortable with him as my employer.

Then, whilst waiting for the last rows to milk out, he grabbed me and slammed his lips on mine. It was a story with a familiar ring to it and though I wanted more, from then on, he left me alone. In the weeks that followed, I couldn't show the same restraint.

On weekdays, dad and mum were at work, and sometimes so was Joey's wife Kat. From our house I could hear his motorbike start up and, in fact, I listened for it. He would normally race down to the cowshed and after a length of time impossible to guess at, he'd come roaring back. I'd make plans to appear in his path. If I had a horse in, I'd saddle up and attempt to align my ride past his house with his return trip. When I struck gold, he'd be burning along, one hand on the fully extended throttle, the other in the pocket of his overalls. He'd laugh like he knew I'd orchestrated the whole thing and look at me like I was the best thing he'd seen all day.

In the beginning, one of those looks would keep me going for hours, but I wasn't always able to put myself in his path. My feelings were disrupting; it was like having boundless energy and nowhere to direct it. My desire for his attention was insatiable. Every cell in my body seemed to strain towards him, and when he'd look my way, those cells gained a sliver of satisfaction for a moment, briefly returning to some form of equilibrium. But the moments of rest and satisfaction arrived unpredictably, so when I didn't get to see him for some time, I'd start running through bizarre scenarios of how I could 'accidentally' come across him. As it would get later in the day and the opportunities for achieving my schemes lessened, desperation would set in, and one night it took over.

Mum and dad had gone to bed. I was in my room, light out, wide awake. Going out my bedroom window might be noisy, creating a high risk of detection, so I opted for the front door, though it was inconveniently situated next to my parent's bedroom. What I hadn't considered, and only realised as I was leaving was, I'd have to lock the front door or leave it swinging in the breeze. I stood outside, my hand on the handle, wondering what the odds were someone would want to get in our house, or the likelihood of the wind getting up. I decided the weather seemed settled, and I was likely the only person sneaking around the valley that night.

Sticking to the shadows, I crept the short distance to Joey's driveway. Because of the streetlight opposite his property, this was the moment I was most at risk of being seen. As I crept down the driveway, sticking to the grass verge so as not to scrunch the gravel, I had plenty of cover; pines on one side and an orchard on the other. I watched intently for movement though because now I was on the property, the enormity of what I was doing was hitting home. If Kat saw me, I had no explanation for being there.

As I got close to the house, I could hear sounds of life. I crouched behind a bush while I made sure there was nobody outside. A little light shone out of a disused front door, diffused through a blind, and I could see Kat on the couch opposite the window, and Joey in a lounger to my right. Both were

43

concentrating on their respective activities. I moved inside the disused entranceway, keeping below the table that sat just inside the window. It was good to see Joey, like I'd been thirsty and had finally taken a sip of water, but it wasn't enough. I needed a long draught, and that meant I needed him to see me. But there was nothing to do but wait.

Time slowed. It was frustrating having to cool my heels, but eventually, Kat left the room. I couldn't see their bedroom windows from inside the doorway, but I guessed she'd gone to the bathroom before heading to bed. I scratched the glass with my fingernail, but Joey didn't move, so I scratched louder. Still, he didn't respond, so I knocked quietly. Frustrated that I still hadn't made an impression, I knocked as if I were at their back door, expecting someone to answer it. Joey suddenly got up, turned the stereo off and walked quickly from the room, switching the light off as he went. Everything went black. I hadn't realised how much light had been coming from the lounge. I carefully moved down the side of the house, but their bedroom windows were also dark. I contemplated knocking on one of them, thinking it might bring Joey outside to investigate, but I knew it could also rouse Kat, so there was nothing for it. I had to go home.

Once I was back in bed, my mind and body raced. I wondered if Joey had known I was there but hadn't wanted to see me, a thought that felt like swallowing poison. I was so desperate it didn't occur to me he might have avoided acknowledging me because the risk of discovery was too high. Now, though, my need was far greater than when the night had begun. I was worse off. My mind and body were screaming at me. I urgently needed to see Joey, to make sure that when he looked at me, it still felt like I was the best thing he'd seen all day.

Several weeks later, I caught a ride to a local party with Joey and Kat and watched things go the way all parties in the valley did. Everyone got drunk. I didn't drink, didn't like the feeling of losing control, so I waited for an opportunity to dance, but unfortunately this party was all adult conversation. Late in the evening, Kat found me.

"I'm heading home to relieve the babysitter," she said.

"I'll come with you." I was assuming Joey was leaving, too. I was tired of watching everyone drink, and if Joey was going, there was no reason for me to hang around. She headed for the kitchen to say her goodbyes and I was following her when someone grabbed me and pulled me into an alcove.

"Don't go—I'm staying!" It was Joey, whispering loudly. It felt risky for him to behave like this in front of everyone, like he wasn't worried, which he then confirmed by kissing me forcefully and walking off like nothing had happened. The room was poorly lit, so maybe nobody saw.

I went into the kitchen, but Kat was already heading down the hall on her way out.

"Kat," I called after her, "I might stay." She paused, suspicion flitting across her face.

"How will you get home?"

"I ... I'll get a lift, don't worry."

Her mouth set in a line as she turned and headed out the door.

The party wound down from there, leaving me waiting, though for what I didn't know, which meant I was vulnerable to the plans of others. A family man who lived a short distance beyond our house insisted on running me home, and I couldn't tell him I'd rather walk because he saw it as his duty to make sure I got their safely. Plus, I couldn't rule out his having seen Joey kiss me. Years later, I came to appreciate his efforts, to see him as the only adult acting responsibly in the situation, but that night, I went on chasing down what I had to have.

When I got home, I waved from the door to confirm I was in safely, then quieted down in my room for fifteen minutes or so, making sure mum and dad were asleep. I didn't dare wait any longer in case Joey had left the party soon after me. I was assuming he'd be walking home; it didn't occur to me my plan would be foiled if he got a ride with someone else.

I snuck out the front door. It was a still night, so no risk of it banging in the wind. When I reached the streetlight opposite Joey's driveway, I tucked into the shadows beside the letter box and waited. Fortunately, Joey hadn't got a ride and must have left the party soon after me, so I didn't need to wait long. He weaved out of the darkness into the light. I waited till he was close, to be sure it was him, and then stepped out of the shadows. He laughed, the sound rolling towards me like puppies emerging from confinement, all so happy to see me. I couldn't help but smile. He walked up and hugged me, then led me across the road to the community hall. He knew where the key was, though I was worried he'd drop it; he was drunker than I'd thought.

We scrambled our way inside the hall at the back and I suppose I expected things to be steamy from that moment on, what with the excitement of such a stolen moment, but he was fumbling around behaving like it was obligatory; he'd promised excitement, and he was going to make good on it. I felt I wasn't enough, like I was doing something wrong, that I should have made him more interested in me, but the reality was he was drunk. He still had a very effective radar operating though, because soon after we got in the room, he suddenly stopped what he was doing.

"She's coming!" I hadn't even registered who she was before he'd pushed me backwards into a cupboard I didn't even know was there. I knew enough to stay completely still though, and of course, I quickly caught on to who was coming. Seeing the flash of light from Kat's torch must have sobered him up considerably, because his performance from then on was stellar. He feigned confusion, calling out like he was unsure of what was going on. Then I heard him stagger towards her as she came in the door.

"What are you doing here?" she said. I wondered how he was going to answer, but he didn't—just acted confused, and it sounded as if she ended up supporting him as they walked out of the building.

I waited in the cupboard far longer than was necessary, just wanting my heart to stop beating so fast. The night had turned into a disaster, had gone from the high of a night out with Joey to the low of there being no opportunity to dance with him, from the stolen moment alone, to facing the reality of his wife and family. Now I had nothing, less than that, complete confusion. I wanted to be with Joey, but rather than it feeling good when I was with him, the way his attention promised, I felt tossed away like a piece of rubbish.

Busted!

Though my relationships, and therefore most of my life, were in chaos, in contrast, I had a good focus on my horses. I was selling one of them and I'd had several calls, with one woman so keen she was driving two and a half hours to see him that morning. She'd told me she'd be at our place between ten and eleven, so I got the horse in from the paddock and put him in the yard beside the house.

I was feeling quite disturbed though. My parents had gone to work, Kat had gone to work, and I'd seen Joey head off to drop his son to kindy, so I knew he'd be back soon. However, I was also aware he'd have to collect his son at midday, and that was what was bothering me. It rarely happened this way. Things didn't align themselves, where he'd be home alone when I was free. I say I, because he never suggested I pop over when he knew he'd be home alone, never appeared down at the cowshed when he knew I'd be milking. I should've noticed that.

By ten thirty, I decided the lady looking to buy my horse wasn't coming. I was freshly showered, ready to go. I figured if she turned up, I'd hear her arrive from Joey's place.

When he answered my knock at his door, I was standing inside the door frame, one hand on each jam. He took a moment to take in the scene, then burst out laughing, causing a shot of pleasure to surge through me. I was glad I didn't have to explain my presence because I hadn't prepared a fake excuse. He walked away, leaving me to close the door and follow him. When we got to the kitchen, I paused, which he sensed. He turned, took my hand, and led me down the hall to the bedroom. When we got there, he drew me in, kissing me slowly and then pushing me on the bed.

You'd think that this moment would be exactly what I'd been waiting for, but this was where he slept with his wife, my friend, so I was facing an uncomfortable reality. Of course, I was also worried she'd turn up unexpectedly, or a neighbour would, and there were no alternative exits. Also, the people from Auckland could still turn up and I was keen to sell my horse.

What I felt but didn't understand till much later was Joey was play-acting. He didn't want to make love any more than I did. I don't know what it was about for him, but I don't believe it was sex. I just wanted to be with him, to have him look at me. I'd have been happy sitting in the kitchen, talking while he made bacon sarnies. It would have achieved far more than the uninspiring tussle we shared.

A few days later, Kat rang and asked me to come over. Though heavily pregnant with their second child, she was working in the garden when I arrived. She barely glanced at me before turning and heading inside, clearly expecting me to follow. Her demeanor made me nervous, not just with fear but excitement too, as if high drama were desirable.

She didn't offer me a cuppa, and as soon as we sat in the lounge, she came out with the reason she'd got me there.

"You've been sleeping with my husband." Of course, said like that it sounded bad, but I'd allowed myself to believe the rumours, that Joey and Kat were swingers, and I'd certainly seen plenty of evidence at parties which suggested they were loose in that regard.

But really, I was so disconnected from reality I don't think I thought anything at all. I was just following my desires. I couldn't explain how I reconciled it. And my feelings didn't change, I was just concerned now with how I was going to continue to get what I wanted. Kat went on calling me out.

"Imagine how I felt Simone, when I came home from work and had to remake my bed. I'm pregnant with Joey's child."

My mind sprinted backwards, trying to think when she'd have come home to a messy bed. How I didn't immediately connect it to the uninspiring tussle a few days earlier, I don't know. I probably believed Joey would have remade the bed after my visit. It only mattered because I wondered whether I was the only one Joey had entertained in his bedroom. Her assumption that it had to be me was disconcerting and I wonder if that was her ploy. I think if she'd asked directly whether I was sleeping with him I might have had the gumption to say no, but as it seemed a foregone conclusion, I admitted it.

Joey spoke to me once more after that, and the most important thing he had to say was I should have denied the affair. I was still only seventeen years old. How was I supposed to know that?

"Comin' Through!"

It would surprise and possibly shock you, to learn Mike was still around after I'd told him our relationship was over. When I stopped working on his farm, my mother stepped in, filling the gap, helping him when she wasn't busy with her day job. Now I had ex-Mike often in my house, and ex-Joey with his very upset wife, just down the road. So, I threw all my energy into training my horse, preparing for an upcoming national event I'd worked hard to qualify for.

The distraction helped me survive because, for several reasons, I was numb. At some point, I'd walked in on my mother in bed with Mike. The room had been dark, so I think she thought I couldn't tell he was in bed with her. I said nothing, not even to my father, and it was some twenty years later before I let her know I'd seen Mike there. I think growing up with certain emotions not allowed meant I didn't know how I felt, or even if I felt. I knew it was wrong, but nobody affirmed that thinking, least of all my mother. People have tried to get me to feel appropriately in relation to it, and I addressed it with my mother once, but her continued suggestion that there was nothing wrong with what happened, caused me to wall it off so I could continue to be in relationship with her. I think the next couple of things I did, though, were deeply connected to what I'd seen, and a destructive way of trying to feel something. Anything really.

Late 80s

Another married friend innocently mentioned she was going away for a weekend, and it spurred me into deciding I needed to seduce her husband. Such a thought process is clearly inexplicable but perhaps a comment a close friend reminded me I'd made once, "you're lucky I don't want your husband," goes some way towards explaining it. My insides were raw. I had to have something to ease the pain, so, the day my friend left I arrived at her door and to her husband's credit, it surprised him to find me there, however he was still ignorant enough to let me in.

Maybe I thought he'd be desperately keen to have sex, but he wasn't. And afterwards, as we dressed, we were silent. I sat on the edge of the bed while he stood in front of me, looking like he wasn't sure where to put himself. There seemed little else to do.

"I'll be off then," I said. He seemed relieved. I was unabashed. I went home and everything was normal. I'd just had a one-night stand with another friend's husband, and everything was normal.

I continued in the same vein. I needed a job to support my expensive sport, but I had to be left with daylight hours to ride. There was a pizza joint that had been one of my favourite eating places growing up, a nice restaurant, not just a takeaway. To get a job there, I figured my physical attributes would do the talking, and I was correct. I dressed in crop top and tight pants, and though I had to come back when the manager was on duty, I completely jumped the queue. And, once on the job, I took an interest in the branch manager Jerry, who, what a shocker, was married, and a lot more proactive than the last guy.

He and I were working a Sunday night together and about mid-evening he got me to come sit with him in the restaurant. Normally, when there's a lull, a couple of staff go on a break together, but it was just me.

Jerry was English, didn't look like he'd ever engaged in much exercise, but he kept slim and clearly liked to look good. He wore a waistcoat and had well-groomed hair. I suppose it was his accent that had attracted me. It reminded me of Joey, and that still felt like unfinished business. Jerry's eyes dominated his face, like his one-word commands dominated during business hours. When customers walked in, he'd call out "do-or" with the second syllable ending in 'o' rather than 'r', or if he were passing between the ovens and the bulkhead he'd call out "comin' through!" The rest of us used the words because we had to—Jerry used them like he enjoyed the impact the sound of his voice had on others.

As soon as I sat at the table with him he said, "I'm gonna ask you something—feel free to say no." I figured it was some sort of proposal, but I wasn't expecting what he delivered.

"Would you like to meet me at the Amarello tomorrow?" It was a hotel on the river, close to the restaurant. He didn't wait for me to show which way I was going to lean.

"I'll book in and ring you in the morning during your shift, to let you know the room number," he said. Woah—he wasn't one for much in the way of wooing. I must have looked taken aback, because he got up, and with one hand resting on the table, looked down at me and said, "Let me know before the end of your shift, okay?" I nodded.

He walked back to the cash register and attended to the take for the night, though he wasn't really concentrating, clearly unsure of what he'd done and what my reaction might be. He was right to be worried because at first; I felt dirty and wondered if this was all I was worth? Clearly, I thought it was, because though I was reluctant, at the end of the evening I told him yes.

I worked my shift the next morning and true to his word, he rang and made some excuse to speak with me. The manager on duty looked curious as he handed me the phone, but other than that, Jerry covered well.

I expected to be excited about things, but I was just nervous. When I walked through the entrance lobby of the hotel, the staff looked at me disinterestedly. If they thought I was there for a rendezvous, they likely saw it all the time and didn't think twice. I was terrified of seeing someone I knew, though it was highly unlikely. During the week, the hotel mainly housed travelling salespeople, but it was Monday during the day, so there probably weren't many of them either.

I knocked on the door. I could hear the television, which contributed to my feeling like a prostitute. Something kept me moving forward though, like I was on one of those conveyor belts at the airport, automatically heading in the direction I was supposed to be going, my efforts contributing towards an inexorable forward movement. It was as if, to get out of what I was intent on doing, I'd have to remove myself aggressively, and I didn't seem to have the wherewithal for that.

Jerry opened the door, looking disheveled. He smiled as he invited me in, though I didn't feel any warmth in it. The room was not as comfortable as I'd expected, given the standard of the hotel. He switched off the television, which instantly sucked the atmosphere out of the room. He wasn't wearing the suit he wore at work, and I noticed how ordinary he looked without it. And old. I wondered how come I hadn't noticed that.

He grabbed his empty glass off the bedside table and asked if I wanted one. He'd brought his own bottles of rum and coke, so he didn't have to use the mini bar. I didn't want a drink, but as it turned out, I probably should have had one. As he busied himself topping up, I put my bag against the wall and sat on the bed. I was still in my uniform with a jacket over the pizza restaurant's distinctive uniform. However, I'd taken off the apron.

Jerry turned, took a swig of his drink, and put it down. I don't think he wanted any more till later. He locked his eyes on me and started taking off his clothes. What struck me was he left his black socks on till the end. He laughed about it, obviously enjoying the juxtaposition and I laughed with him, but I didn't think it was funny. He looked absurd. If I were looking for a little romance, I was in the wrong place. Then he stopped and just stood looking at me. I was supposed to follow his lead, which I did. He moved in, wrapping himself around me and tipping us on the bed. I wish I could say things heated up for me, but they never did. I doubt it was much better for him, but he'd paid for the room, so I think he was determined to get his money's worth.

When we'd finished, he lay back with the sheet over his waist and lit a cigarette. Somehow, that was the most attractive part of the whole thing. With a cigarette in his mouth, he looked like the man I saw at work most days. Maybe that was important to notice, that attracting the man in charge was the most satisfying part of the process.

"Are we gonna do this again?" he asked, which surprised me. I thought it'd been disappointing.

"If you like ...."

"Did you ... like it, I mean?" I'm not sure I had many options at that point in terms of a reply.

"I did—I was just nervous." He seemed okay with my answer, nodding before taking a long drag on his cigarette.

We sat quietly for a minute. Then he took another couple of quick drags, stubbed the cigarette out, threw off the sheet and started getting dressed. I slunk out of bed, grabbing my clothes from the floor, and heading for the bathroom. When I came out, he'd put his jeans back on and was smoking another cigarette.

"Are you going?" he asked.

"Yeah, I think so ... you?"

"I'll stay for a while, watch a little television."

I nodded and bent down to pick up my bag. He followed me to the door and put his body in the way so he could kiss me. Then he opened it and let me past. I hadn't gone more than a few steps when I heard the door clunk behind me.

Elephant in the Room

So, pizza guy Jerry and I became an item, and as I understood it, his wife didn't know. Not because he hid it well. I figured she just didn't care. Or possibly I told myself that to justify my position—however unjustifiable. Jerry said little about her, so it wasn't hard to forget she existed, except for the telling issue of being unable to go to his place. I still lived with my mother, who'd left my father by this point, so my place wasn't an option either. We ended up hanging out at work or in his car, though he wasn't averse to going out to dinner, as if he thought it was unlikely anyone would see us. I wondered why I was more concerned about being discovered than he was.

Inevitably, our easy avoidance of his wife ended abruptly. He and I had spent another evening out together and returned to the restaurant so I could pick up my car. Jerry parked next to it, but we fell into a deep conversation, and it only occurred to me later that time must have slipped away.

His wife's souped-up car roaring past on the street roused us, and all credit to him, Jerry was quick to react.

"Get out—it's Lena!" I moved fast, grabbing my jacket and frantically searching my bag for my keys. I unlocked my car door as Jerry called out final instructions.

"Lock the door and pretend to be asleep!" As I slid into the car, I slammed and locked the door, put my head on the rest, and faced away from the window.

We'd parked our cars behind the restaurant and, undoubtedly, after finding the front door locked, Lena must have hopped back in her car and roared around the back. On finding our vehicles there, she parked straddling the rear of both, got out, leaving her engine running, and started banging on Jerry's car door. He acted as if she'd just woken him, reminding me of a similar situation not so long ago. Then she turned her attention to my car.

You can't be ready for this. You can play the game, usually wearing one hell of a poker face, but I don't think you're ever prepared to face the consequences of your actions. I'd already heard her tear into Jerry, as any wife would, and I could feel the pressure of her eyes on the back of my head. She banged on my window, but I held my nerve. I feel fortunate she felt little need to waste time on me. I think she could see the writing on the wall. Jerry wasn't worth the effort.

When it was clear I wouldn't respond, she yelled at Jerry to follow her, jumped in the car, foot flat to the floor and almost failed to stop when she reached the entrance to the road. Jerry dutifully started his car and followed her.

As the sound of their engines trailed into the distance, I folded my arms across the steering wheel and laid my forehead on them. It was obvious I knew nothing about their relationship. My sense of her disinterest was only a reflection of his behaviour and nothing to do with reality. I felt like nothing; a mistress, yes, but nobody runs around announcing that. In fact, it seems it's the most unacceptable behaviour a woman can engage in.

I put the key in the ignition and drove home through the deserted streets, the occasional set of oncoming headlights letting me know I wasn't the only person left in the world.

She left him. Without a backward glance, it seemed, which should have worried me. In the same way she'd appeared disinterested in his life, he started living separately from me, keeping things to himself. I was now openly his girlfriend, yet I didn't find out about any of his three flat mates till they'd moved in. He didn't even have a conversation with me while he was considering it. Or it could have been a spur-of-the-moment decision, which he failed to mention. Either way, it was a telltale sign we were running parallel to each other.

Eventually, it got me down. He'd hold parties saying nothing about them to me beforehand, then wander around wearing only an elephant G-string and his black calf-length boots. And he'd laugh at me because I found this embarrassing. Everyone else's reaction was, "aww Jerry," good-naturedly long-suffering, even though they'd seen it more than once. To me, it was getting old, beginning to look childish.

And unfortunately, his loutish behaviour extended to the bedroom, taking one particularly degrading instance of this to bang the final nail in the coffin of our relationship. He laughingly claimed to be remorseful. I didn't leave him physically right then, but I did in every other way.

Death Wish

2006

As it got closer to the end of the year, it became commonplace for me to be at church or hanging around with Paul and Marie, in group settings, or with either of them on their own. They seemed comfortable having me there, yet I sensed a trap was being laid, but not by me. Rather, I was the spring securing the plate, waiting for an unsuspecting Paul to put his weight in the wrong place.

It was a Tuesday morning at church, and I was downstairs in the café with him. There was an ease in our relationship now, and like most people who spent time with him, I was laughing a lot, or deep in conversation about the things of God. Certainly, I enjoyed it, though I suspected more so than was healthy for me. As we sat enjoying our coffee, there came a noticeable change in our conversation.

"So then, I was wondering how much work you want to do here at the church," he said. "How many hours would work for you ... and Steve?"

I was immediately wary. Things at home were tentative regarding the commitments I was taking on at the church. I supposed the admin staff were looking to use me more but wouldn't want to come to rely on me if I couldn't commit, so Paul was trying to get a feel for the situation.

"I'd like to do more, but my son's kindy is only twice a week, plus the distance from home, and coming across on Sunday and other times during the week. I think doing more would get to be a bit much."

His countenance drooped. "Well, we really appreciate all that you already do," he said. He looked down and then smiled up at me. I thought he was going to head back upstairs, but obviously there was more on his mind. "I have some unofficial work for you though, if you're up for it?"

Because of my past behaviour, I think I knew what work he was going to have for me, but I didn't want him to show his vulnerability. I knew I was good at my maneuvering, that I'd created the conditions where he felt he could lean on me, and I felt a tinge of guilt at the way I'd taken advantage of his sweet nature.

"What's that then?" I said, awaiting the inevitable.

"I wonder if you could help me understand my wife."

I wanted to push his request away, not have to make the choice he'd just put before me; help him like he asked, or disappoint by telling him no. Yet, alongside my distress at what I considered a serious faux pas on his part, was my sense of success in having the object of my obsession come to trust me so explicitly. The telltale excitement revved in the background. Paul had just put his weight on the plate and the spring had tensed.

He needed a response, so I answered, the words coming out of my mouth feeling completely foreign, like I was spitting gravel.

"I don't think I can help. I don't know if I understand her."

His response was alarming. His eyes flashed and lost their normal gentle expression. He seemed to suspect I thought less of him for asking, or he had some sense I was running away, which frustrated him. He couldn't understand why.

"You're a woman, and women understand women, don't they?"

I wish I could have allowed Paul to make such a mistake and get away with it. That would have been the truly loving thing to do. But what he'd just asked was like a freight train running through me. I could feel the weight of it pushing me down the track.

※

It's funny how things that seem so obvious to you are not to others. I thought everyone knew that if a man looks to you for help with his wife, he's in trouble. It's classic husband stealing fodder. He may not be aware of it. In fact, mostly I believe that's the case, but he is falling fast unless something or someone alters his course for him. With womanly wiles, it's a gold medal winning performance. Or maybe I'm wrong about that? I don't know how I knew it, or why I felt it was so obviously true. Even now, I don't know if it really is a thing, however, even if I felt guilty for having done it, I also felt I should've been taking a victory lap.

※

There'd been a simple end-of-year lunch for the church staff, at a lovely café in the middle of a quaint, rose filled garden. I'd dressed carefully, so it should have been obvious to me I had intentions. Then a few days after the lunch I'd sent what I thought was an innocuous email to Beth, thinking I'd spoken to her about much the same stuff in earlier emails:

> Hi Beth, had a bit of a battle with God tonight. I mentioned in my last email about that innocent staff lunch with Paul, and now I've seen it wasn't so innocent.

I spent my time trying to manipulate him, to attract him ... whatever ... I told God I don't want to stop. I know it leads to death, but I don't want to stop. So, I was shown more, that even before I met Paul, I'd decided I would control him.

I was referring to a meeting I'd all but forgotten, which had occurred before I'd joined Paul's theology class, before I'd ever even met him. It'd been the night our home church had gathered, and the announcement had been made the group was going to be wrapped up. It had shocked me, given I was clueless the change had been coming. The home church was my community, my lifeline, and my connection to Beth and without it, I didn't know if she'd still be in relationship with me. That thought had been devastating. Her husband Dean had told us the reason the group was ending was because we no longer had leadership in Auckland willing and capable of running it. Then he'd presented what he thought would solve the problem.

"We have good friends in Paul and Marie Bowen. They lead a local church. A lot of you know Paul. He's taught at some of our conferences in the past and he's well respected throughout the country. He's been suggesting for a while you all join him at his church ... and I think now's the right time."

Following the announcement, I'd struggled to think straight, and when the formal part of the evening had ended, I'd sat in a lounge chair out of the way, attempting to process things. I was trying to gain some traction, just observing everyone else and letting my thoughts flow. As I processed, there'd been a moment of comprehension, a realisation that I could salvage the situation, which at that point had felt dire. It had been just a spark, but it was enough and as the details of what I needed to do had come to me, my distress had dissipated, and the more I'd pondered my solution, the more obvious it'd become. So, with the means apparent, a calm had come over me, like I'd punched a program into a computer and all I had to do was wait for the program to run its course.

While I'd been processing, the evening had come to a natural end around me, so I'd headed for the front door. Beth had been in the office talking with Dean and another couple and I'd caught her eye as I'd walked past. I think she knew I was distressed. I believed she should have known the impact the announcement would have on me and warned me it was coming. I was consoling myself though, having decided she wouldn't need to concern herself anymore because I had everything in hand. As I'd thought about Paul, this church leader I'd not yet met, and apparently a teacher of some repute, a steely resolve had risen in my heart. I knew what had to be done.

The email to Beth was in front of me, cursor flashing. I went on keying, telling her that all those months earlier, on the night Dean had announced the end of our home church, I'd designated Paul as my target. I had vowed to myself and whoever else was listening, "I am going to own him."

That I'd decided I was going to own Paul even before I met him should have been a major red flag to me. But I was oblivious to the fact it was a statement any different to what I'd shared with Beth previously, so her decisive response shocked and even frightened me:

> Hi Simone, I would like to chat with you on the phone—can do approx. 1.30 today if that is a good time for you?

I would like to suggest that you stop this. The first step is to stop your work on Tuesday—no more. You give notice that you will not be available. You have other commitments that you are getting behind on—you are not to say, but one of them is walking away from this kind of behaviour and thinking. And you need to let go of ANY OTHER committee or involvement you have with the church, apart from attending as a member of the congregation on Sundays.

... You can be a princess in the Kingdom of God, but we all serve someone. We can choose whom and keep calling ourselves back to it. With Jesus, you have already received the most love, and all your needs are met in Him if you will do it His way, and not trust yourself to do it the way you have been.

Love,

Beth

It's Your Choice

Following Beth's email, I was sick for two weeks, which obviously wasn't the real reason for backing off at the church, but it was the formal story I gave. However, in that I hadn't yet built up the courage to tell Paul I wouldn't be able to work there anymore, when Marie asked me to go in on the third Tuesday, I felt justified to do so because it was Paul's wife making the request. However, I was watchful of my motives, and kept my distance from Paul, which may have been what drew his attention.

I'd been up in the office with a couple of staff and had kept to myself, focusing on the work and not engaging the way I normally would in case I slipped up. Paul had been in and out of the office, but I'd been quiet, so he'd had nothing to respond to, but close to lunch I popped downstairs to put up notices in the café.

Minutes later, I heard Paul padding down the stairs to join me. Beth had warned about assuming someone's motives, but I couldn't help but feel flattered he'd made the effort, even though he had a legitimate reason to be there; he had more notices for me to put on the board.

"How're you doing?" he said, brow furrowed.

"I'm okay now—it was just a cold." I turned back to the board to pin up a notice before stepping off the chair.

"You still sound pretty stuffed up. Are you sure you should be here?"

"I was worried they might dock my pay." He laughed, and I reminded myself to tone it down, knowing it was best if our meeting didn't gain traction. I walked over to where I'd left more notices to go on the board.

"Here's a few more," he said, following me. As I took them I met his eyes, yet I knew I shouldn't, but I didn't want him to experience me differently and feel he'd done something wrong. He smiled, and the empty place inside me instantly flooded with warmth. It felt like life to me, and I wondered for the hundredth time how it could be wrong. However, I tried to honour my arrangement with Beth by giving him no encouragement, and therefore no reason to hang around, so after checking how my family was, he popped back upstairs.

On Sunday, as I drove to church, I was scanning. Since Beth's email, each time I'd thought about Paul, I'd called myself back to my relationship with the Lord, yet there'd been no comfort in it. It was hard maintaining such a rigid structure, so I easily fell back into familiar patterns, checking oncoming cars, looking for one make, model, and colour, and then checking the number plate. When it wasn't Paul's, I'd resume my scanning.

I stormed into church and, like a pinball bouncing from person to person, I couldn't connect. Paul was there. I'd clocked his position as soon as I'd walked in, but I refused to look at him, performing a clever mind trick whereby I blamed him for my neediness. I had my son with me, so I deliberately focused on him, which was probably a shock as he was used to my attention being constantly divided. I felt sorry for him for that, yet powerless to prevent it.

I took him up to the mezzanine floor and was working hard at concentrating on him when Paul arrived at the top of the landing.

It was impossible to avoid meeting his eyes, and I smiled, or thought I did, but he didn't smile back, so maybe my smile had looked more like a grimace. I turned to my son, told myself I had to keep my eyes on him. Paul went into the admin office, and then I heard the door on the landing slap as he headed back downstairs.

I hated treating him like this, felt him silently questioning me. In the past, when I'd told Beth about it, she'd growled, querying why I felt responsible for his feelings, or why I thought he needed me to help him feel good about himself.

"You can't go there," she'd told me. She kept sending me back to the Bible, had me digging deep in the book of Romans, and of course I wanted to be dead to sin and alive to God (Romans 6:11), though maybe only because of what I didn't want. I didn't want to hurt my husband, or my son, didn't want to disrupt or possibly destroy Paul and his family, or the church. So, I spent time in the scriptures, and sought God, even in my unbelief, and help and relief came in various guises.

A good friend of Paul's and another renowned bible teacher, Matthew, came into the church to do a few sessions. The opening line of his first message rocked my world.

"It's in relationship that we see," he said. It prompted my recollection of a conversation I'd had with Paul at work during a coffee break. We'd been sitting in the café chatting away, enjoying each other's company, or so I'd thought, but without comment, Paul had abruptly stood and left.

I'd panicked, wondering what I'd done wrong. It was so unlike him to be rude. I'd tracked back through our conversation to work out what might have caused him to act that way, but as Matthew taught, I realised I hadn't been enjoying a conversation with Paul that morning. I'd been flirting with him. On the surface, I'd been acting as I did with many others, having a bit of fun, bantering, but the intention of my heart had been to capture him. I'd wanted to position him in such a way that I could bend him to my will. What hit hardest in this revelation was the description of flirting that Matthew gave later in the lesson.

"It's the promise of sex, with no intention of paying," he said.

Being unable to engage in my usual maneuvering was painful. The ache in my solar plexus never let up. I believe it was grief; I denied myself what I knew would sate me, and that felt like a loss. Yet I determined I'd sit with the pain and not fix it, which was a new phenomenon for me, to have a need and not attempt to fill it. And Beth told me how to get through the pain.

"Allow God to work with you," she said. "Yield to Him. Keep talking with Him and listen and respond as He guides."

Sitting with the pain, allowing it to flow through my body, sent me into a downward spiral, like someone had pulled the plug out of life and I was being sucked down the drain. Nothing was enjoyable or took my mind off what I was feeling. All I knew was emptiness, the pain of it, but I wouldn't let myself escape. Beth was pleased I was in pain.

"Truth is guarded by problems, and He doesn't give it to us lightly," she said. "I used to think it was because we couldn't handle it or wouldn't value it as part of His way of living, but now I think partly, the pain comes because God is taking us through it, and our experiencing it helps us to be in the reality of Him more."

It went on for months, the pain, and I noticed it created a spaciousness in me. I thought the space was just that, but on the contrary, it came with a sense of solidity. And I noticed I cried more easily for myself and others, as if letting myself feel my pain was deepening my compassion.

In the middle of it all, I had an incredible phone conversation with Beth, which felt like I could talk to her about anything. It was as if I'd settled into a feather down quilt, fully supported, every inch of my body received by the soft material. Maybe the Lord had flowed into the spaciousness created in me, so there was less of the fleshy stuff coming between us. Indeed, I felt so accepted I told her about a needy trip I'd made into the church.

"Did you get it?" she said. "What you needed?" I assumed she wanted to know if I was being encouraged by Paul, but later I realised she'd just wanted to draw my attention to the futility of my behaviour.

"No, I didn't," I said. "I think I learned what hooks me, though."

"What's that?" she said.

"It's the need to be needed. Paul is always so thankful for anything I do. It doesn't have to be much."

"It's good you see that's a hook," she said. "But you know it's not about you, don't you? What you do, Paul is thankful for."

I intellectually understood that was the case, but I didn't own it, wasn't living it. Helping him made me feel worthwhile. His appreciation affirmed me.

"You are not all," she said. "You need to see that and not get pumped up by what you do. It's for God's glory, not yours."

I think that was where the rub lay. I still wanted the glory for myself, needed to feel someone important saw value in me. And probably that was the crux of it. I was valuing man's opinion over God's.

At the end of our conversation, I had a burning question, yet I wasn't sure I was ready to hear the answer, as if being ignorant was a safer place to stand.

"How long do you think it's gonna take me to get through this?" I said.

The fact I asked suggested I believed I could get through to the other side of my battle, which was progress at least. However, I think I expected her to at least pause while she considered her answer, that the solution would be as difficult as I was finding the problem. But without hesitation, like a machine gun, she fired her answer at me.

"6 weeks, 6 months, 2 years—you choose."

Theme Revised

Late '80s

Horses cost a lot to run. I needed more money than I could make as a waitress, so when I spotted a job with glide time—negotiable work hours before 9am and after 3pm—I applied, thinking it would give me the flexibility I needed to ride before and after work.

I got the job and started at State Insurance the day after Cyclone Bola struck. It was one of the costliest storms ever to hit New Zealand, which meant I didn't get to meet the inspectors for days; they were out in the community assessing the damage. Which wouldn't ordinarily have mattered, but as life would have it, it delayed my meeting the subject of the next chapter in my life.

The inspectors relayed what seemed to be fantastical stories. A 30-foot yacht in a tree, sheep in trees, and cars floating out to sea—probably cars in trees, too. The claims staff had their heads down, taking calls from distraught clients, and even the new business team had to lend a hand. They sat me at a desk, quickly taught me how to do some simple work, and left me to my own devices.

I was still seeing Jerry and working at the restaurant occasionally; however, the way I felt about myself was tentative and two of the young men I worked there with had intervened with advice that would have been difficult for them to give. They must have noticed I'd been purging in the staff toilets or seen what Jerry was up to, which I'd yet to discover. However, they couldn't have known how mercenary my approach had become. Jerry and I were planning a trip to Hawaii, which he was paying for, and I was intent on getting my free holiday. As far as I was concerned, once that was over, so was our relationship.

At the end of my first week at the insurance company, I was finally introduced to Steve, the Senior Inspector. There was another inspector called Steve, which confused me for a while; I didn't know which one had which surname. But during tea breaks when they played pool in the staffroom, only one of them attracted my attention, particularly as he leant over the table to take a shot. Still, other than noticing his pool table maneuvers, I had little to do with him until late in the year when he got a promotion, which made him my boss, and that always seemed to be an attractive quality.

Steve was often at the center of things, moving easily from solving work issues, disappearing into an office for a senior management meeting, or sitting on the corner of a desk talking about the meaning of life. I couldn't imagine anyone more capable. His response to every query seemed to flow effortlessly, whereby he'd answer you directly or ask a question that helped you find your own answer. I was in awe, to the point of distraction, and as I later learned, one of the other managers had noticed my declining performance and mentioned I'd gone off the boil. Really, though, I was boiling hard. I was just on a different element.

Even after my free trip to Hawaii, I still lunched at the restaurant occasionally and during one of these I caught on to what my two young advisers had probably been aware of, and which Jerry hadn't mentioned. Sierra, friendly, all quick action and clipped sentences, had filled my waitressing shoes by taking on the daytime shifts on Mondays and Tuesdays. It only took a moment of carelessness on her part for me to see she'd taken on more than my shifts. I was standing at the bar looking into the bulkhead where they make the pizzas, and Jerry was beside the ovens waiting for the cooked pizzas to come out. Sierra walked through, heading for the kitchen and, as if she didn't realise I was watching, or possibly because she did, she sidled up to Jerry. When she was almost touching him, she lifted her knee against his thigh. Jerry laughed and moved away, strongly resisting the urge to glance in my direction. He was painfully aware I was watching.

It was too late; I was already so distant from him I wasn't seeing anything through rose-tinted spectacles. I calculated what I'd just seen, a possessive gesture showing much more than a working relationship, and I made my decision. I wasn't going back. I just had to pass that information on to Jerry.

He invited me out to dinner, probably because he'd noticed how distant I'd become or was worried about what I'd interpreted in his exchange with Sierra. He was attentive, and I played along, but afterwards, as we paused at traffic signals on the way back to our cars, I let him know I didn't want to see him again. Because the evening had been so pleasant, I think it floored him. His eyes widened, and he begged me to reconsider, but the harder he begged, the more resolute I became. Even his crying had no effect. I walked away, leaving him alone at the lights.

I wasn't much of a one for taking a breather. So, when at any given moment, I knew where Steve was in the office, or he smiled at me and my senses sang, I knew that once again, the horse had bolted. Thinking about him fueled a constant energy when he wasn't around and a degeneration into a speechless gorm when he was. I recorded every move he made and every look he gave for dissection and analysis later. But there was nothing to be done as Steve gave no sign he intended acting on the attraction, which I believed was mutual, of course. I had to. It was the only way my imaginings sated my need.

It would have been good with Jerry no longer in my life to say the new year brought with it a new freedom, but at work, I was busy monitoring. I'd be loading insurance on the computer, typing, eyes on the screen, but when someone approached Steve's desk, my attention would be on what was going on around him. If Steve left his desk, which was a couple behind mine, I'd hear him move, and I'd employ every sense I had at my disposal to keep abreast of where he went in the office.

Things were no better outside the office. When I drove around town, I behaved as if I might see him at any point. It didn't matter that he lived in the opposite direction and would have no reason to be on the same roads as me. I still checked every car coming towards me, and even more far-fetched, when I was at home, I checked every car that drove past. To put that in context, I lived twenty-five minutes from town on a road that didn't go anywhere other than further into the valley. If I was watching television, I'd jump up and look out the window. If I was out the back, I'd rush to the front of the house to check who it was. If I was working my horse, I'd turn my attention to the road for a moment, while I made sure the car going past wasn't his. All this watching, my 'scanning', made me feel alive, the possibility of unexpectedly glimpsing him continually spurring me on.

Mid to late January, the subject of the movie *Dirty Dancing* arose in the office.

"I've got it on video," I said, happy at the thought of watching it again for what would probably be the twentieth time.

"We could get together at someone's place to watch it," Megan said.

"When? Tonight?" Jane didn't sound overly keen; she wasn't really into socialising with her work colleagues.

Megan nodded and turned to Steve. "Your family's away—how 'bout at yours?"

Steve looked up, feigning a pained expression. "How did I get dragged into this?"

"Come on ..." Megan said. "You know you want to."

"I can come," I said, trying to help things along, especially now Steve was involved. One of the young guys mentioned he could make it, too.

"So, it's at Steve's then, about seven." Megan looked at him for confirmation, and he didn't say no. She waited a moment and then rolled her eyes. "So, what's your address, doofus?"

Steve reeled it off, and those who were interested made a note of it. I counted five of us.

Of course, I dressed deliberately in tight pants and a crop top, mentally trying to will the others not to turn up. When I arrived there were no cars in the driveway, which boded well, and when Steve answered the door, he told me Megan had rung to say she wasn't coming. Jane and the young guy just never showed. I was pleased, but the optics of our situation made things a little tense.

Steve was wearing tan shorts and a white tee-shirt that sported a cheeky surfing cartoon about the Exxon Valdez, and I liked the more relaxed look, but it was difficult to reconcile it with my picture of him as my boss. He asked if I wanted a drink and, as he had a soft drink, I asked for the same. I looked around while he was in the kitchen. The house was ordinary, and the evidence of Steve's life outside of work was everywhere. I'd passed his daughter's bike in the carport. There were photos of the family and one or other of the kids dotted around the living room, and there was clearly a woman's touch in the soft furnishings and decoration.

Steve came back with my drink and exchanged it for the movie, which he loaded on the VCR. The movie played straight away and once I'd settled on the chair, Steve lay on the couch. When the movie ended, the video went straight into *The Princess Bride*, which I'd forgotten my uncle had loaded on the tape to fill it up.

"Shall we watch this too?" Steve asked with the machine on pause. I just wanted to be in the same room with him. I didn't care.

"Yeah, why not?"

By the end of the second movie, I was tired but also sorry it was over. There were the soft murmurings of good night as if we didn't want to spoil the atmosphere, and when I got to the car, I sat for a moment assimilating all that had happened.

I could still feel the emotion of the two movies, the unacceptable relationship in *Dirty Dancing* and the satirical love story of *The Princess Bride*. Then there was the emotional strain of being alone with Steve for four hours. It was a heady mix, and I glowed in the ride, totally oblivious that things in the emotions department were gathering themselves for a sharp U-turn.

I headed for the bypass and as I skirted town, it suddenly occurred to me Steve had made no sort of move towards me, even though we'd just spent four hours alone. He'd been less friendly than at work, where we bounced off each other's cheeky repartee. The conversation during the movies had been concise, stilted even. I didn't doubt his attraction to me and maybe I should have, but I was confident I'd read the signs and figured it was obvious I liked him—crop top, tight pants—so what was wrong?

Something was different in a way I didn't understand. Of course, some things were still the same: he was married, and he was my boss. I believed he found me attractive, and I'd arranged for us to meet in circumstances conducive to us getting together. I don't believe he could have thought anything other than I was interested, which left me with only one conclusion. He'd denied himself, which was the one thing I didn't want to believe. If I couldn't get him to do what I wanted, then I wouldn't get what I needed. At that point, reality set in, and the truth flashed in front of me in neon lights. I hadn't been able to get this man to enter my imaginings.

It was a moonlit night and as I reached the southern end of town, close to my turnoff, nestled between a couple of sheds sitting on the edge of the river was a gap, and as I floated past, I glanced left, out over the river towards the road on the other side. I glimpsed the full moon reflected off the water, and I took a screenshot in my mind's eye. Yet, it wasn't the only thing I captured. I heard something, not audibly, but in my heart. And I didn't hear it so much as I received it. An understanding, a revelation, the wall between me and a whole aspect of human understanding suddenly removed.

What came to me, in part, was there was a way to live. And for the first time, it had revealed itself in a form I could comprehend and instantly apply to myself. It wasn't some booming voice overriding me, but it had spoken gently to my heart. I wasn't afraid, nor did I feel condemned. I was just surprised. How had I been unaware the world wasn't there to do my bidding, to be manipulated by me? That I wasn't free to do what I wanted, not because of the harm I might do to someone else, though in time I learned that was important, but because of the world's arrangement. There was an unchanging force, not a set of rules, not guidelines I could choose to follow or not, but a law like gravity, operating whether or not I believed it, and whether or not I knew it was there. I'd been living life, taking what I wanted to meet my needs with little regard for anyone else, and in that moment, I could see I'd been trying to fight this law; to walk off the cliff and think I wouldn't fall to the ground. I didn't know whose way this was, but at that moment, I was painfully aware it was irrefutable.

I immediately began scrambling to take back what I felt was slipping away from me. I thought of Steve at work, how I could almost feel the warmth of his body when he'd glance my way. His blonde hair, blue eyes, six-foot-two frame created a physical presence that had me, and I noticed a few others metaphorically sheltering under his arms. His ability to distill every business situation into a simple solution brought with it a sense of surety and safety, something I was so desperate for. I was fighting for my right to control it; to take hold of it so I could arrange for my need. I could hear myself making my case, justifying my position, complaining about what I hadn't had, didn't have, and still needed.

But this way stood in front of me like a sentry. It didn't move or crowd me; it just presented itself. Once I'd seen it, all I wanted to do was un-see it, to go about my business the way I always had. But in its light, I couldn't. It exposed the very intentions of my heart. If Steve had made a move on me that night, I would not have hesitated to steal him from his wife and family, to assert my rights as I perceived them. And now I could tell that option was no longer available to me.

I was driving through the industrial area of town now. The only other vehicles on the road were trucks. Tears fell, blurring my vision and soaking through my top. Until then, I don't think I'd ever really cried for myself. The tears were for the things I didn't have that I should have, for the lack in my life causing me to want what it was I couldn't have, for, though I thought it might be within my power to take Steve, I couldn't, not in the way I wanted to or had done in the past with other men.

The world as I knew it had come to a grinding halt. Yet it was my decision. I hadn't felt forced, and it wasn't out of any altruistic sense of protecting Steve or his family, but to protect myself. Suddenly, I had value in my own eyes that I'd not had before. It was like some unknown benefactor had just gently nudged me towards a better way to live.

Sucker Punches

Still, at work, I went on getting my fix every day. Steve was my boss, required to be there and interact. Not that I think he objected, but I could tell the attitude he'd had at our private movie night had not altered. He was still actively keeping his distance. So I enjoyed being around him within the bounds of propriety. There were the smiles exchanged as we passed in the stairwell, intimate times in the passageways between filing cabinets, where I could feel the warmth of his body moving past as we carefully avoided touching. These little moments were teasers keeping my obsession ticking over. However, eventually the situation had to come to a head.

That day was unassuming in its beginnings. I had to find a file in the archives, and with our building previously housing a bank, the files were in the old vault on a floor below the office. Staff accepted that looking for a file could take a while, some of them were in order, but often you'd do a good deal of searching before you found the one you wanted.

The vault was eerily quiet, every sound amplified. I sat on the floor and made myself comfortable. The only sound my fingers flicking through the files. But then came the unmistakable clip of shoes on lino, and someone breathing. I was busy hoping against hope that it was Steve when he appeared around the corner holding a file, like he was there on business, but I suspected he was looking for me.

"Hi," he said, "any luck?"

"No ... not yet." I turned back to the files, though I wasn't registering what I was seeing. He said nothing, but I could feel the burden of what he wanted to say. Finally, with the moment loaded with expectation, he spoke.

"We really need to talk about this, don't we?" he said. I bit my lip and quickly nodded, giving him no reason to think there was any hesitation on my part. He named a café nearby and suggested we meet there at lunchtime. I managed an 'okay' and he smiled. "See you then," he said.

I listened to the clip of his steps as he walked away, my mind a haze of wonderings. What had just happened? When had it become okay to concede there was something going on between us? And considering my moonlit night revelation, why had I so easily accepted his invitation?

At lunchtime we left the office together, which hadn't been part of the plan, and a curious look from a co-worker reminded me of our tentative position, though Steve seemed unperturbed. The coffee shop was below street level, in the centre of town, so it was busy. We grabbed something from the lunch bar and sat at a table for two set against the wall. I chose a single sandwich, thinking I wouldn't be able to eat. Understandable because I'm a woman, but Steve did the same. We settled in, and he managed a few mouthfuls before the drinks arrived. Once the waitress had gone, it seemed he was ready to get down to business.

"I wanted to tell you I've left my wife," he said.

I wasn't expecting that. I wanted to cover my face with my hands, to think without an audience. He'd been so clearly taken away from me after the movie night at his house, and now suddenly, the circumstances had altered.

"There's something going on here, isn't there ... between you and me?" he said, carefully placing his sandwich on the plate.

"Yes, I think there is."

I could feel the sense of gravity. I held his eyes for a moment and then let the contact drop, unable to handle his intense scrutiny. He took a sip of his drink, placing it carefully back on the table. I still had eaten nothing; it would have been like chewing polystyrene.

"I wanted to ask about your situation with that guy from the restaurant?" he said.

It surprised me he knew about Jerry, but it wasn't like I'd been quiet about the trip to Hawaii or my waitressing shifts. I was pleased to hear he'd taken an interest, though.

"Oh ... that. Completely over." I wanted him to discount it and get on with what he'd come to say.

"Can I let you know where I'm at then?"

I nodded, but was totally unprepared for what followed.

"I can't have kids," he said.

It was like I'd been sucker punched. He'd been unavailable, suddenly available, and then the whole concept of him and me cruelly sabotaged. Everything in me ground to a halt.

"I had a vasectomy last year," he said.

Wow, did he realise the impact he was having? I'd barely taken in the news of his availability, and now it felt like he was being snatched away again. His attitude was so final, like he was determined not to have any more kids.

"When?" I asked, without knowing why I wanted to know.

"October." So, only three or four months earlier.

"You had no concerns about your marriage back then?" I was watching him closely, trying to glean as much as I could.

"Well ... yes I did." He looked a little deflated, "I just don't want any more kids."

So, it was final. I had to admire his candour; he was laying it all on the line, clearly not looking for a short-term relationship. It bothered me he couldn't have kids, perhaps a sign I'd been thinking long term too. Not that kids were on my mind, but I'd always assumed that would be available to me. However, I did the only thing I could in the circumstances. I blew right past it. On offer was the object of my obsession. I'm not sure I was in any position to turn him down, least of all over an issue that, at that point, wasn't on my radar.

"That's okay ... it doesn't matter," I said. He queried my answer, and I assured him I meant it, but the issue should have carried more weight, for both our sakes. At twenty, I was too young to know what I was saying goodbye to, but he'd already had two kids with a wife who'd worked overtime on him to get them. Granted, at that point he didn't know about the baggage I was bringing with me, or that it had just fueled the impetus to override the issue but, in that he'd put it out there up front, it was clear he was aware of the hazards involved.

When we left the café, he had promised nothing, had made no arrangements to see me again, and had given no definite idea of his intentions. What he had given me were two pieces of new information; he'd left his wife, and he didn't want any more kids, which, in being shared, spoke volumes.

Days later, I stood at the door of Mum's house looking across the paddocks, past the barn that hugged the edge of the road, and the cowshed on the corner, to the one lane bridge beyond. In the front paddock, Monty, my dun gelding, was grazing quietly. He was the most promising horse I'd ever owned. When he moved, he floated, his action dreamlike, and when he jumped, he rounded his back over the fence, performing a perfect arc from take-off to landing. Looking at him was a mouth-watering experience and just seeing him grazing peacefully created a sense of calm and normalcy. But on this day, even he couldn't hold my attention. Several cars came around the corner, over the one lane bridge speeding down the metal road towards our house, but they weren't Steve's.

Since our lunch at the café things at work had been the same, yet I was more peaceful, fortified knowing that Steve did in fact have feelings for me. Yet I still didn't really know what was going on. There'd been no further acknowledgment of the feelings we had for each other, no private conversations. Nothing, until now. I watched as a white car bounded off the one lane bridge, and my hand, which had been holding the pendant of my necklace, dropped to the door handle. The car sped past the T-junction by the cowshed, dust and stones flying as it reached full speed past the barn. Then I heard the engine slow, and my heart clenched, used to the many disappointments this sort of moment had produced in the past.

It didn't matter that the vehicles coming down the road moments earlier hadn't been the one I was looking for, or indeed, all those other times when I'd systematically checked every vehicle going past the house, because today I'd known for sure, eventually one of them would be his. I watched intently as the white Camira pulled into the driveway. I took a deep breath, pushed down on the door handle, and walked out to meet him.

The Deal Breaker

My friend Dianne once asked, why Steve? How, when I clearly had a revolving door issue with married men, did I know he was the one I wanted to marry? Aside from the obvious, that he was the only one who left his wife prior to starting a relationship with me, I think about who I was during that time in my life. I was looking for safety. I'd felt exposed and unsafe on an emotional level for a good proportion of my life. Steve represented a haven. Physically, he was six feet, two inches tall, so he was the arms I could shelter under, but I have indeed seen several women do that with him literally, so clearly he presents as caring and protective. He also had an accurate compass regarding the direction to take in any situation, had a wisdom I felt I could trust, like he'd always take the right path. Ultimately, though, he gave off a vibe that he'd rip a person's head off if they attempted to harm you, and I like that about a man.

Late '80s, early '90s

I didn't miss a beat. With Steve having left his wife, I decided that meant he wasn't married anymore, so in my fledgling understanding of the way to live, he was now available. My previous relationships had begun while the men were still with their wives, so I considered this to be completely different, and in that Steve appeared to believe the same thing, I felt secure.

We rented a one-bedroom flat from someone Steve knew, and we carried on working at the insurance company. I kept on with my horses, and Steve with his football. Then, after a few years, we bought a dairy farm with my mother and Mike. They'd formally become a couple at the end of my parent's marriage. I lived with the discomfort of my mother being in a relationship with my ex by fencing off the relationship I'd had with him. I doubt it's possible to do that, but in that I imagined I could, I managed.

The dairy farm was fifty-eight hectares of largely rolling countryside on the east coast, tucked away in its own little valley. It was milking one hundred and twenty cows in a twelve-a-side herringbone cowshed. I left the insurance industry to run the farm and not long after, Steve and I made plans to get married.

Our engagement had happened quietly a few months after we'd got together, so marriage had been a long time coming. I was now twenty-five years old. However, talk of marriage again raised that Steve couldn't have children and with the first flush of our relationship now worn off, I was no longer blinded by my obsession. I faced the reality that marrying him would probably mean not having children, something I'd always thought I'd be able to do. So, that was one issue, plus the cows began calving six weeks after we arrived on the farm, and I was suddenly deeply immersed in farming life.

The intensity of the upsurge in work meant I was alone a lot and exhausted when Steve was around. Initially it was fine, but as time went on and the farm work became more monotonous, I wearied, and with Steve resentful at how often he had to pitch in, the compounding pressures pressed on my vulnerabilities. I found the storehouse of feeling loved, which in my case really meant feeling attractive, quickly depleted and ran into the negative zone.

It was the first time since becoming a couple that our relationship came under threat.

The farm work also exacerbated some of the back injuries I'd sustained falling off horses and one nasty flip off a motorbike when I was seventeen, so I started going to an osteopath for treatment. He was an older man, but sometimes he got in a young locum. Tim was chatty and enjoyed talking about the kayaking he did. In fact, he did his kayaking on a river out past our farm, which meant he was regularly driving past. It was a piece of information that caught my attention, and I popped it at the back of my mind for future reference.

Tim took an interest in me, and I liked that. It made me feel special or, to be more precise, attractive. Our weekly half-hour sessions became a bit of a lifeline amid the drudgery of the farm work, and the tenseness of my relationship with Steve. As Tim worked on my back, he talked about his interests and listened to the things I liked to talk about, and because I was getting off the farm, it meant I could also dress up and feel like a woman again.

But half an hour a week wasn't enough, and I hungered for more and true to past form, I formed a habit of watching for Tim's vehicle driving past the farm. I took every opportunity to head up the race. Putting electric fences up, bringing in the cows. It all meant I got to watch for Tim's vehicle, and even though this watching went on for weeks, I only spotted him once. Still, that was enough, and I happily anticipated telling him at my next appointment.

"I saw you heading out to the river on Monday," I said as soon as he'd settled into his work. "I was up the race bringing the cows in."

His hands stilled. I thought he'd be interested that I'd seen his car, but the way his hands slowly went back to work, like his mind was busy searching through files of data, seemed to suggest something else.

"Man, you must lead a sad life—to have the time to notice my car driving past."

It took a moment, but I quickly recognised the sentiment behind his comment. It was pity, maybe even a wary pity. The warmth at my sense of our mutual enjoyment of each other turned cold. I was glad I was lying face down on the table so he couldn't see the effect of his comment. I felt sick in the pit of my stomach, and as he chatted away, I just made appropriate noises in the right places so he couldn't tell I was upset.

I left his surgery with my tail between my legs, cheeks burning as I played his "sad life" comment over and over. I was so sure he'd share my pleasure in having spotted his car that I couldn't see it as the outside observer did. I lived in a world where I was a star, the object of someone's desire. Somehow, I believed my having spotted him was supposed to please him, but clearly, it'd done nothing of the sort.

Yet even though he'd knocked me back, at my next appointment I just fronted up for more. Tim was curious and talkative and that led him to ask questions about my life. He'd noticed the tension levels in my back, and his probing for cause eventually came around to the subject of my marriage, and on from there to the fact that my husband couldn't have kids.

"That's a deal breaker, isn't it?" he asked.

I was sitting on the edge of the table, my feet not quite reaching the ground, wearing a floral summer dress that accentuated my curves in all the right places. I was fit and toned from working on the farm, so I'm sure I was quite the picture. I looked down at my feet and swung them back and forth.

"I don't think it's quite that simple," I said. I could feel the heaviness developing in the pit of my stomach again.

"I think it is," he said. "He should get the vasectomy reversed or cut you loose."

Man, he'd switched from preachin' to meddlin'. I pushed myself off the table and walked over to the chair where I'd left my bag. He was leaning over the desk, writing notes in my file.

"But I love him," I said, just into the air, more to reassure myself than anything. He stopped writing notes, straightened up, and looked at me.

"How great is his love for you, though? That's the question really, isn't it?"

I grabbed my bag and reached for the door handle. The heaviness in my stomach moved, became an ache in my chest. Tim didn't seem to notice I was literally running away from him. As I walked back to my car, I wondered whether he was right, and it really was that simple. Was it less about my love for Steve and more about how much Steve loved me? For the first time, I let myself think about what life would be like without him.

That night I rang my friend Tessa and told her how immovable Steve was regarding having kids. She had a son and another one in the offing, very much amid attaining what I thought I desired, and I felt she knew who I was in the situation, and Steve. I told her about Tim, about our intimate conversations and how, based on those conversations, I thought he liked me. I told her we'd talked about my marriage, most notably about Steve not wanting to go the extra mile to have kids, and that Tim had been damning on the subject. Finally, I let her know he'd given me his home phone number, and based on that, I'd assumed there was some sort of connection between us.

What I didn't tell her was it had taken some planning on my part to wrangle his phone number out of him. I'd considered calling the ladies in reception, but I knew it wasn't something they'd just hand out, so I'd used a little feminine manipulation to get it straight from him. And I think the fact I had his phone number swayed my friend Tessa into thinking along the same lines as me; that there was something going on. And like Tim, I think she agreed the kids' issue was a deal breaker, so her counsel that night reflected that belief. I told her Steve wasn't budging, so I was leaving, and her last comment as I remember it was, "Go to Tim." I wonder now whether I just heard what I wanted to hear.

I didn't know where Tim lived, so I called him and a woman answered—not a good sign, though I could hear what sounded like a party in the background, so I assumed she was a guest. I asked if I could speak to Tim. I could tell it was hard for her to hear me, but once she had, she dutifully went to get him. It left me with the sounds of the party and then eventually Tim's voice on the end of the line.

"Hello" he said. I could hear a slight irritation in his voice.

"Tim, it's Simone." There was a long pause.

"Simone?" he said and then the sound of the receiver being bumped or him putting his hand over it for a moment. "What are you calling me here for?" he said.

I went blank for a moment and then my mind ran, leaping through the files I had on each of the intimate moments I believed we'd shared. He'd given me his phone number. How did he not know why I was calling him there?

"I'm leaving Steve," I said, carrying on with my original intent even in the face of the fast-mounting evidence that I might have read things completely wrong.

"Why are you telling me?" he said. Now I was really confused. My mind couldn't run fast enough. But Tim knew exactly where things stood. "You need to go back and talk to Steve," he said, "sort it out with him." I'd exasperated him, annoyed him. My life was sad. This was so not going the way I'd imagined.

"But I thought ..."

"No, Simone, no. Talk to Steve. I've got to go. I'll talk to you later." He left me with the dial tone.

I put the phone back on the cradle and dropped onto the hallway floor. There was a blank space where my mind should have been and, in sensing my distress, our two Rottweilers rose from whatever wall they'd been holding up. I hugged them, dragging my sense of worth up from whatever rock it had crawled under to consider what might have happened to them if Tim had encouraged me to follow through. I buried my face in their necks and Tango pushed in on Cash. They both began growling, a dispute over who should be closest to Mum.

Steve came home that night, and I told him nothing of what had occurred, and we lived a few more weeks like that, but the peace at any cost couldn't last. We were maybe eight weeks from our wedding. Previously, I'd felt as if he held all the cards in our relationship, a telling way to look at things, but now I had to gather my strength and resolve, which was easier now that I'd concluded we might not stay together.

I knew I had to be careful how I approached the issue, tell him how I felt so he didn't refer me back to the conversation about kids we'd had all those years earlier. Logically, he would know it was a low thing to do, to hold me to my acceptance of the situation back then, but logic didn't come into things. He was determined not to have any more children; I might almost have said he was phobic about it.

We were in the farmhouse kitchen with its horrid, puce coloured wallpaper and cracked lino. The décor perfectly harmonised with my state of mind.

"Steve, we need to talk about having kids."

As soon as the words were out, the black cloud descended. Not that it'd been that far above us, as the atmosphere was already strained for several reasons. I was managing the farm on a subsistence level wage, so money was tight, and any money the farm made was being fed straight back into the property. We'd purchased it in a rundown state, and it had been part of the agreement going in that we'd reinvest everything to bring it back up to scratch. But Steve was unhappy with the lack of income, as well as how much he had to help on the farm because Mike wouldn't spend any extra money.

I can see now that all round, for Steve, there really was no upside. He'd have to go through surgery to have the vasectomy reversed, and he didn't want any more kids. Really didn't. He was already experiencing difficulties with his ex-wife around visitation with the two he had, and looking out further in time, if we got pregnant, he'd be the sole breadwinner for a while as well. And, from experience, he'd seen that one kid wasn't enough, that women normally wanted more. It must have looked to him as if there were no bottom to the situation, just a continual free fall. So that was the increase in the layers of tension at the mere mention of a conversation about it.

"I just don't want any more kids," he said. He was standing at the bench making a coffee, preferring to keep his eyes trained on the revolting wallpaper, rather than look at me. I knew such a position wasn't good for ensuring a profitable conversation, so I changed tack.

"Can we sit in the lounge and talk?"

He turned slowly and looked at me, then went back to what he was doing. I knew my best option was to head down there and hope he followed. He went about it slowly, but eventually we ended up in the lounge sitting on the seventies suite Steve had inherited from his parents. It was one of those faux leather ones with the orange cushions. The lounge room had yellow loop pile carpet that had seen better days a decade ago, and all the windows were at a similar height to the mantle that sat over the inoperative old fireplace, so the only view you got when you sat down was of a dead fireplace and the tops of the trees outside.

"What are we gonna do then?" I asked.

"About what?" he said.

He was so tiring when he took the evasive 'you forced me to do this, so you can suffer' stance.

"About me wanting kids."

"What can we do?"

Okay, fair cop, I was going to have to be the one to float the obvious option.

"So, do we call it quits, then?" I said.

Now it was out there, it felt good. Like we were getting somewhere instead of skirting round things like we had been these last few months. He just looked at me for a while.

"How would we go about it?" he said finally. I think he thought, or hoped, that my mentioning splitting up was a bluff, but it hadn't been, and I had to show him that.

"Maybe you could find a place in town?" Yep, that surprised him. He paused.

"Is that what you want?"

"Nope—I want to have kids."

We'd reached an impasse, but now we both knew where the other stood. I had to have the guts to leave Steve in this position, not rescue him by backing down, but I didn't want him to stand there alone. I suggested he call his sister, and then I took the dogs and left, went down to the cowshed where I didn't really have anything to do. I just wanted to give him room. I'd had time to process the possibility we might have to end our relationship. He hadn't. When I came home about an hour later, he'd gone.

Now, with everything up in the air, I was alone. I often was, but not when I was experiencing such strong emotions. My friend Michelle rang and great friend she was, dropped everything and came straight out to the farm. I didn't want to talk about the situation so much as have someone there with me, and Michelle instinctively knew this. She didn't push too hard to find out what was going on or ask how I was feeling. She just told me she was staying to help milk. I don't know if I showed it, but I was incredibly grateful and relieved to know I didn't have to do it alone, not in the state I was in.

Someone else in the shed at milking time is a real boon. It takes all the pressure off. One of you gets the cows in while the other sets up the shed, and when the cows get to the yards, you can push the first row in the bails and have the cups on by the time the other one has shut the gate behind the herd and dropped into the pit.

Plus, during milking, you can pop in and out of the shed without worrying about what's going on with the cows while you're gone. And milking flows more easily. Someone can go out in the yard to bring the cows into the bails, while the other one's pushing them up. Otherwise, you're up and down the stairs, in and out of the pit, just trying to bring a row in. And then when you've finished milking and the last row is heading up the race, one of you does the machines while the other hoses the yard. It's just a more relaxed process.

But though Michelle was there, lessening the pressure of the job, the angst I was feeling ramped up tenfold. I was in panic mode. Had I done the right thing—did I really want children so much I'd sacrifice my relationship with Steve for the opportunity? I couldn't even be sure of that. And my need to ease Steve's pain, to tell him not to worry, that I'd do without kids, pressed on me heavily.

As we got to the last few rows, I periodically hopped out of the pit to look down the driveway, or out to the road. I calculated how long Steve had been gone and what that meant in terms of his decision-making process. Of course, I couldn't know what it meant, but that didn't stop me from making calculations. Eventually we finished milking and after shutting the gate to the cow's paddock, we returned to the house and Michelle left.

When Steve got home, he told me he'd made his choice. I'm not sure what I expected the outcome to be, but I don't think I thought there'd be a result straight away. I imagined a few weeks of Steve wrestling with himself over why he was so averse to having more kids, so for him to tell me he'd decided made me suspect bad news was coming. I prepped, waiting for the axe to fall.

"I'll have the operation, reverse the vasectomy," he said.

It was the second time in as many weeks that my mind blanked. His determination not to have kids had been with us for so long, I wondered how a resolution could have been so easy.

Reality Check

Early 1994

Steve and I married as planned and yes, I had my reservations. I knew I hadn't dealt with the obsessive behaviour, that it sat just below the surface, awaiting its next target. Yet I probably couldn't have articulated that if I'd been asked. The knowledge seemed to sit just outside my immediate reach, like I was hiding it from myself. So, unfortunately, once we were married, things quickly slipped back to where they'd been. I reverted to type.

It was summer now, the days long and hot, the heat shimmering off the corrugated iron roof on the hay barn and the cows all desperately seeking the shelter of trees, or milling around the trough, waiting for their turn to drink.

One morning after milking, I dressed like I was going to the beach. I had no intention of doing so. It was a ritual to trick myself into believing my intentions were pure, or I just wanted a plausible explanation if it became necessary. I wore a bikini I'd bought in Hawaii when I'd been there with Jerry, and I pulled on a summer skirt to keep it seemly. I hopped in our little yellow Mitsubishi which, by that time of the morning, was steaming hot, threw a towel and a drink on the seat beside me, and then paused. Was I really gonna do this? I sat there with the heat building up in the car, and without knowing whether I answered my question or just had to get moving, I turned the key in the ignition and headed out to the coast.

Everything was legitimate so far. If questioned, I had all the right answers. I'm not sure why I thought anyone would ask, but if they did, I was just an overheated farm worker going to the beach to cool off. Nothing odd about that, other than I rarely went to the beach, and certainly, if I did, I would never go alone. I was a nervous beach goer, always questioning whether I'd correctly identified the rip, or whether there was something dangerous lurking beneath the waves. I knew approximately where I was heading, though I'd not been there before, only heard via the grapevine where Joey lived. It didn't take long to get there, maybe fifteen minutes, which is perhaps why I did it. If he'd lived further away, I doubt I would have.

I hadn't seen Joey since he'd told me I shouldn't have admitted the affair to his wife. I didn't know how I was going to see him and even if I did, I couldn't know the reception I'd get. I could well imagine how Kat would react. Her parting shot a few months after she'd outed me had been an attempted punch at a local party. Fortunately, thwarted, first by the cramped conditions preventing her gaining any power in her swing, and secondly by the anticipation of the party's host who'd recognised trouble was arising, had seen I was about to retaliate and had been there to pull us apart.

I found the road I'd heard that Joey lived on. It was right by the water, so the bikini option was a good cover. The street had houses on either side, all designed to catch a view of the water, the ones opposite the beach elevated to do so. I drove to the end of the road, turned, and parked on the beach side, opposite the house

I suspected was Joey's. I turned off the engine and wound down a couple of windows.

As soon as the engine went silent, I felt exposed. There were no other parked cars and all the houses had huge windows facing the road, so I imagined, to the people behind those windows, my car would stand out like a sore thumb. They'd be wondering what I was doing, probably thinking I was casing the joint; a thief doing their due diligence. In fact, they could have binoculars on me right now, and be taking down the number plate. My biggest fear was Joey or Kat would figure out it was me sitting there, and I'd never know they had. They'd respond to the situation, take some action to counter what I was doing, like completely ignore me, and there I'd be sitting, waiting, wanting something to happen while they moved on with their lives.

I considered my options. I could start up the car and drive away, which in the face of feeling so exposed held quite an appeal, but then it would make the whole exercise of dressing up and driving down a waste of time, so that wasn't immediately acceptable to me. I'd come here because I wanted something, and being here, waiting for it to happen, gave me hope I'd receive it. There was another obvious option: I could sit and wait. Yet that was worrying because I was almost expecting a cop to come cruising down the road at any moment, and, if Joey or Kat used the binoculars, they might recognise me. Finally, there was a third option; get out and head down to the beach. But that made no sense. If I'd wanted to go to the beach, I would have driven right up to it further down the road, not parked here and headed down via the access this end of the street offered. So, in the absence of a clear winner, the second option won. I just sat there waiting for the circumstances to make my decision for me, which, conveniently, they did.

I heard a noise coming from Joey's house. Perhaps it was a door slamming because a figure appeared, a boy, maybe eight years old. He had dark hair and wore typical boy wear for that time of year, a pair of board shorts and a t-shirt. He walked down the driveway and as he crossed the road, his walk morphed into the tight rope style of someone attempting to protect their feet from the stones. As he passed in front of my car, he stared into the vehicle, and I stared back. He looked angry, his thick, black eyebrows becoming one as they furrowed across his forehead, and I realised I'd seen those eyes before.

He had to be the child Kat had been carrying when she'd questioned me about the affair. This boy was his father's son, the spitting image of Joey. He was real, not a part of any scenario I'd created in my head. His eyes were questioning, asking what I was doing there, and I felt embarrassed, like a much younger sibling had caught me with my hand in the cookie jar. I don't know whether it was guilt or shame which caused me to react, but suddenly I had to go, and fast. As the boy continued down to the beach, I started up the car and stuck it in gear. I didn't even look at the house as I drove away. I turned onto the main road and headed home, trying not to think about what I'd just done, which didn't work. I knew exactly what my intentions had been, and I couldn't stop thinking about them. As I drove past all the houses that vied for pride of position in terms of sea view, I chastised myself. And when I got home, there was plenty of reality waiting for me.

When it came time for milking, I slid into my track pants, the oil of the milk ingrained in the material that pressed firm against the front of my thighs, the unmistakable odour of off milk wafting up to my nostrils. I jumped on the four-wheeler and headed up to the cows, feeling the pings on my shirt as the bike's fat wheels hit fresh cow pats and flicked it onto my back. Once the cows were in the shed and I was milking, if any of them relieved themselves while I was standing in the pit a metre or so below their hooves, I was in the splatter zone. Now, all of that was reality. I don't know what I'd been thinking.

But my little trip to the beach caused me to acknowledge my limitations. I couldn't continue working on the farm, I knew that. I was too alone; it was going to force me into making a big mistake. So that's what I told Steve, that I was too lonely for this life, which didn't worry him. He wanted out anyway. I think continuing to have Mike as an influence in my life was proving too uncomfortable for him. So, Mike bought us out of the farm, and we purchased a lifestyle block further up the road. Now I had to get a job, which I did, with another of the big insurers in town, and I went back to the nine to five.

The Confession

Mid 1994-1996

It didn't take long for the nine to five to pall. One evening after work, waiting out the front of the office for Steve to pick me up, I began expressing my concerns about the bind of working a job to workmate Leanne.

"We get up, we go to work, we come home, we go to bed—day after day," I said.

"Yeah, but what else is there?" she said.

We were standing just off the street in front of the entrance to our building. The concrete was wet, the air damp, and the light fading. Even though she'd said 'yeah', I wondered if she agreed, as she often played the foil, making me unsure of her real opinion.

"There has to be something—I mean, there's got to be more to life than this?" I said, raising a hand, sweeping it out towards the surrounding buildings, but I think what I meant was how purposeless it all felt.

"What if there isn't?" she said.

Not something more than this? It shocked me it was even a thought on the table. Did this lifestyle appeal to her? She wasn't playing the foil and didn't object to the way things were? I couldn't imagine it, but faced with her questions, which suggested acceptance of the status quo, I felt more hopeless and helpless. We cut our conversation short when her husband pulled up to the curb and as they drove off; I noticed that though our conversation had ended, my ruminations hadn't.

Then one day a man came into the office. He was short and dark, and unremarkable looking. Normally there would have been someone else to attend to him because I was part of the administration team, not customer service, but it was morning tea-time, so I was covering. I'd already begun making my way to the counter when he spotted me. I smiled, and he returned my smile, placing the parcel he was carrying carefully in front of him and, like most people, leaning on the counter which stood at chest height, designed for the purpose.

"How can I help?" I said, standard fare in the insurance business, unlike the vibe I was picking up from this guy. He was unusual, the air thicker around him, making me more aware of myself moving through the moment. His eyes appeared merry and danced, leading me to engage with him at a deeper level than I normally would have.

"I am here this morning to insure my new car!" He said it with a flourish, as if he'd just waved a magic wand. Normally such theatricality would have been off-putting, but his manner had drawn me in, so I laughed with him instead.

"That's easy then. Do you have any other insurance with us?"

"I do," he said.

"Another car?"

"No."

I placed a form in front of him and handed him a pen, taking his details so I could find him on the computer. As he wrote, he gave a running commentary about his name, his address, his year of birth. Normally that might annoy as we don't need those extra details, only the bare facts, but with him it seemed like part of the show. Now and then I noticed he would put his arm on the parcel he'd rested on the counter in front of him, like maybe it gave him a sense of security, or he was just making sure it was still there. It also occurred to me he may have been trying to draw attention to it. Eventually, he couldn't seem to help himself and held the parcel up to me.

"Do you know what this is?"

The parcel was the shape of a book. I didn't want to tell him I knew what was in the parcel, not only that it was a book, but also its title. I didn't understand how I knew—only that I did. I shook my head, no, and I can't really explain why I lied. He looked knowingly at me, his eyes heralding the moment he seemed desperate to get to.

"It's a bible," he said. I feigned surprise, not telling him I had indeed known that. And now he'd got the information out, he seemed to calm down. He completed his paperwork, and after exchanging a bit of banter with some claims staff who were returning from their break, he left, surprisingly quietly. I noticed that my time with him stayed with me long after he'd gone.

Around that time, Steve received a call from Henry, our old karate teacher, wanting to come around with a friend to chat about a business opportunity.

"It's bound to be network marketing," I said in a phone call with my mum that afternoon, and I was right.

They bounced into our house that evening and we liked what we heard, but mostly we liked Henry and his friend. Their excitement was infectious. So, we took the "fork in the road", a common quote in "The Business", and got involved. It didn't seem like a big thing, but it began a connection with a group of people who became like family. They wrapped us up and wouldn't let go.

We started listening to tapes, all Australian and American accents, telling stories about letting the boss know what he could do with his job, or pulling your Lear jet up in someone's driveway to rub your financial success in their nay-saying face. We read books it'd never occurred to us to read, paradigm changing, self-help books like *The Magic of Thinking Big* and *How to Win Friends and Influence People*, and in a short time we began seeing the world differently.

Yet the business was also all that people accuse network marketing of. It had several cult-like qualities and was all American rah-rah, which, in non-Kiwi fashion, I just loved. There were huge meetings several times a year with thousands of people from all over New Zealand. I'd seen nothing like it before, with massive queues to get in, followed by an all-out free for all to get to the front seats. And the functions lasted all weekend, running into the early hours. Then it'd start all over again at nine or ten that same morning. These were intense times, which had a huge impact on the people we were. But for me, one morning had the greatest impact of all.

I knew the Sunday morning sessions were like church. We'd been told they held them so that regular churchgoers could still attend a service while they were away at functions. I'd turned up because of a specific invite from one of our leaders, coupled with a strong sense I needed to be there. Steve had taken the opportunity for a sleep in. The whole atmosphere differed from the night before, the rah-rah replaced with reverence, people leaning in quietly to speak to others, an awareness that some people just wanted to sit alone, and a personal desire to be quiet, meditative even.

I found a seat on a bleacher at the back. There were far fewer attendees than at the main sessions, so I was on my own there. It was dark, a long way from the stage lighting, and the exit doors had velvet curtains blocking the light. Darkness was good. I didn't know what went on at these meetings, so it felt safer.

The guy speaking was American, of course, and tiny. Well, short and slim, but probably for an American, not tiny. His hair looked blow-dried and styled, like he was some fifty's throwback. To add to that impression, he was wearing a turtleneck jumper underneath a sports jacket, probably appropriate in America, but here it looked like my Nana had dressed him. However, there was no underestimating his talent. When he began singing, he sounded like a burley African American, and I waited for the real owner of the voice to appear from the wings.

Then he brought his message. He talked about eternity, something I'd not considered before, which was surprising. I just never thought about what would happen to me after I died. My thinking centred more on what would happen to me when I got old, who would be there for me given Steve was older, and men usually died first. I'd wondered how I'd support myself, and that had been a big part of the reason I'd wanted to get in the business, attracted to the passive income it promised.

The preacher was well into the meat of his message, busy suggesting different ways people think about what happens when they die, and after each explanation he'd say, "Well, that might be right." He even spoke about how I'd approached it, calling it the "bury your head in the sand" method.

"Well, that could be okay. Maybe it's not worth thinking about," he said.

I wondered where he was going with the message, in that he was suggesting any of the ways of thinking about it could be reasonable, and he hadn't shot one of them down. But then he produced the clincher.

"But what if you're wrong?" He let that sink in for a moment and then added, "Eternity is the wrong thing to be wrong about."

Now he'd certainly attracted my attention.

He asked everyone to close his or her eyes, which I did, though I didn't like it, as if someone might creep up on me. It changed the atmosphere in the room, and I thought no more about eternity, didn't get the opportunity. Something else was going on; I was not alone. Not in the normal way you think of, because the room was full of people, but internally, which I considered baffling. But it was undeniable. The only way I could describe the internal presence was it had a way to it, a solidity.

A quiet came over the whole auditorium and the preacher insisted we keep our eyes closed and our heads bowed. Then he asked a question, and those who wanted to respond were to raise their hand. My arm shot up, not in any way half-hearted, and although I knew I was going to put my hand up, the vehemence with which I did was a surprise. Part of me wanted to reach up with my other hand and pull it back down.

The preacher was commenting on the hands he was seeing raised all over the auditorium, and it was comforting to know I wasn't the only one, but I was glad I was up the back, in the dark. Music filtered through the room. The preacher commented again on all the hands and then asked those with their hands raised to stand. Now he really was attacking my inhibitions, stretching me. I did it, though I opened my eyes. He asked us to move to the front, just below the stage and everything in me refused, but the unfamiliar presence moved me forward, and along with what looked to be a hundred others or more, I made my way to the front.

Once there, the preacher led us in a confession, having us ask Jesus into our lives. Things got a little chaotic after that. A guy broke down, not just crying but sobbing his heart out, and I could hear a commotion a little further away where people were just falling over like a wave had swept through the crowd, but for me there was serenity and security. I felt full, like I'd had a flaccid balloon inside me, and someone had just blown it up. It was a sense of wholeness I'd never known, and in that moment nothing else mattered.

Then Steve was there, wrapping me up. I tried to explain what I thought had just happened.

"I know, I know, it's okay. I wish I'd been here," he said.

Then we just stood there in each other's arms, crying, oblivious to all that was going on around us.

It's hard to reconcile that moment with what followed as the Sunday afternoon session began revving up. I might have called it a counter punch. The music was throbbing, and people were gathering in groups in the aisles talking intently about what they'd learned, and all they were going to do to get this business built once they got back home. Unfortunately, it was always more difficult to motivate yourself once you'd left the safety net of the function. Steve was busy talking with some others and I felt a need to be alone with my thoughts, so I left the auditorium.

The preacher from the morning session was standing in the foyer and people were waiting for the opportunity to meet him and chat. If there was one thing the business did well, it was edification. All weekend they'd have touted from the stage that talking with the speaker would have been of great benefit to the success of your business. So, the crowd gathered and waited.

I stood back for a moment, wanting to join the line, but I was unsure. The next couple walked up, and the husband shook hands with the preacher, and the wife briefly hugged him. All three talked animatedly, and I wondered what they were saying, how they knew what to talk about. I watched as the preacher greeted a few more groups of people, and then I joined the line, still unsure of what I was going to say to him. I wasn't even certain why I wanted to meet him, other than the presence of a worrying feeling that, if I didn't, I'd have missed out and let myself down.

As I moved closer to him in the line, I sensed the preacher could see me coming. Our eyes met several times. He seemed a little curious. I could feel the familiar surge of adrenalin at the sense of power that gave me, as if I wanted to take hold of, or control, the purveyor of what I'd experienced that morning.

When the couple in front of me walked away, his eyes briefly followed them and then fell on me. He was leaning against the table that held the tapes he was selling. I'd already bought a few sets over the weekend. He folded his arms, which seemed defensive, and I switched from feeling powerful to feeling judged and deemed threatening. This man thought I was dangerous.

He didn't move or say anything, just held my gaze. I was going to have to make all the running. I held back for the briefest moment, completely unsure of what to say, and when it was obvious he wouldn't rescue me by leading the conversation, I jerked forward, my arms outstretched.

"Can I have a hug?"

There was an awkward moment as he weighed his options, but slowly, he moved forward into my embrace. Don't tax yourself, buddy, I thought.

"Okay," he said, smiling and extricating himself. Not quickly, but the hug had been tense. I smiled back at him, but now in the face of feeling judged, I couldn't wait to get away.

As I walked back towards the auditorium, I could feel the heat in my cheeks. I knew they were flaming, plus I was fuming. Who did he think he was? Short American dressed by his nana. I veered away from the double doors of the auditorium and headed for the toilets. I was going to need a moment.

Targeted

1996-2004

I didn't understand all that had happened to me at the function, and though there was some attempt by people in the business to connect me to a faith group, what I'd experienced quickly moved to the back of my mind, leaving my dissatisfaction with life to flourish.

I decided the problem must be the place I worked. I'd been there a couple of years, had banged heads with my immediate supervisor far too often, and because I wasn't one to just put up with things, I quit and went back to State. I knew it wasn't a highly satisfying move, just a side-step to put me in more familiar territory. We didn't think it would be for much longer anyway as we'd thrown ourselves into building our networking business, and we hoped it would set us free from work, me first and then Steve.

Eventually the business released me to a degree, though it took several more years and didn't happen the way we'd imagined. We sold our house and with the proceeds sitting in the bank along with what we earned from the business, we could bring me home from work as a decision made for us as a family, rather than for financial reasons. I was in my early thirties now, so we'd decided it was time to have a child, however that might look.

It's hard to understand me making such a major decision when I was still hedging my bets, making sure I could grab the attention of other men when I needed it. I just didn't have any sense of solidity; I was in a constant state of flux. However, unbeknownst to me, people capable of helping with that were being moved into position.

We'd met Billy, the leader of the networking business, in a busy carpark in 1995. Someone had told us he was a large man, yet that had done nothing to explain what it was like being around him. Yes, physically he took up a lot of space but his attention on you was attractive, made you feel you were the most important person in the world. As he'd walked through the crowd towards us that day, he'd glided, his nimbleness seeming out of place, given his size. He'd worn an affable expression, shaded variously by the cutout pattern of his golfing hat.

"Gidday," he'd said, in a classic Aussie drawl.

He'd asked how long we'd been in the business and whose group we were in, acknowledging our line of sponsorship, "that's a good group," before moving on to speak to others.

It was a year later, one night after a function, when friends invited us back to his hotel suite. It was wall to wall people. Billy sat in the centre talking about his time in the business, and how he'd been able to rise to one of the pinnacle levels of success. However, I got the impression the business wasn't his favourite subject, and noticed he soon turned the conversation towards his faith, a subject which set my wariness radar off, especially when people bubbled up amongst us, laughing for some inexplicable reason. Billy and others prayed for people who then fell over, which I thought was incredibly strange, and I had a strong urge to escape. Yet as quickly as the mystical had begun, it stopped, and in the same way I'd not understood why it'd started, I couldn't see why it ended either.

It must have been about two or three in the morning when people finally filed out of the room, off to bed, but it seemed Billy hadn't finished with me and Steve yet, and he drew us aside to chat. I'm not sure how much of the chat I heard because my body started shaking like I was a can in the grip of a paint shaker, and the more I shook, the more vulnerable I felt. Billy moved in close and said something, but all I could think about were his eyes. They were so blue, and they just wouldn't let up their pressure. Then he blew on me and I swayed, panicking at what felt like a complete loss of control. Billy grabbed my arm, reassuring me, then he let me go and blew on me again.

I don't know how long I remained focused on only what was going on within, but long enough that when I opened my eyes, most people had left the room. I was lying on the floor where I'd fallen after Billy had let me go. When he saw I'd come to, he got down and lay mirror image in front of me.

"You've got really blue eyes, you know that?" he said. It seemed completely out of place, but years later I connected it to the thought I'd had before I fell, about how blue his eyes were.

From that point, his influence in our lives grew. On one trip to Malaysia, we met him in a parking garage with, strangely, not a car in sight. It was all rather claustrophobic, with solid concrete above and below.

"You're not gonna fall, are you?" Billy said.

"No," I said, adamant I could stop myself. But when he blew on me, the power of it dropped me to the ground, not like a tree falling, more like someone had punched me. Billy and Steve had tried to grab me, but I'd fallen so fast they'd both missed. I was unhurt though; poleaxed onto solid concrete and unscathed. I didn't know what to make of the falling, but in that I'd attempted to prevent it and failed miserably, I suspected God might have been involved.

We were becoming close with Billy and his wife Pauline, spending time with them around functions, and at other times, too. When Billy learned that Steve's vasectomy reversal a few years earlier had been unsuccessful, and that we'd decided other methods of getting pregnant were not for us, he suggested we look at adoption. We did and entered the adoption pool soon after. It wasn't long after we'd shifted to Auckland for a better job opportunity for Steve that the birth mother of our son chose our profile. Four days after we'd received the joyous news, he came to live with us, though the formal adoption happened a year or so later.

It was at an Australian function in the Gold Coast a year after that when I noticed a change in the air, that things in our life were heating up. Something was coming. It was a Sunday morning, the time when the downright unexplainable often occurred and I had the feeling this Sunday would not disappoint. Greg Burson was the speaker, known as a prophet, which meant little to me. It was merely another one of those odd Christian expressions I'd avoided during my non-religious upbringing. But I trusted Billy, so if he thought Greg had something to offer, I was completely open to it.

Prior to the session, I was standing outside the auditorium taking in enough caffeine to get me through, when I noticed a group of men coming towards me. I knew most of them, but as they got closer, I saw they had an older guy with them. He had a slightly offbeat, surfer type vibe. The group was moving quickly on their way somewhere and not wanting to give the impression they had time to stop and chat. As they swung past, I caught the eye of the surfer guy. I meant nothing by it. I was just interested because I hadn't seen him before.

He met my eyes and held my gaze, hard, if that's possible. As they arced around me, it was as if he threw out a line from his eyes to mine and hung on for dear life. I don't believe I could have dropped the connection even if I'd wanted to. I felt he was reading the story of my life in those brief seconds, a conduit taking in the information, for what purpose I didn't know. It was one of those moments you highlight, forget, and move on. It only becomes useful considering the events that follow.

Steve found me and we went into the auditorium just as things got underway. Greg was speaking, and I wasn't surprised he was the surfer guy I'd seen in the entranceway. I expected the look he'd given me earlier to prove meaningful during his message, but it didn't. I knew it was important, though, and I slipped back into a watchful state.

Close to lunchtime, the session finished, leaving me a little deflated. Steve and I were at the back of the auditorium. I was still hoping something would happen, though it was becoming increasingly unlikely. We could see Billy and Greg over the other side of the room, deep in conversation, so it seemed there wouldn't be any chance of catching up.

Then Billy looked up and glanced around, clearly searching for someone. He leant in towards Greg and spoke, and they turned and headed our way. They passed clusters of people, and I kept expecting them to stop at one or other of them, but Billy was on a mission and heading straight for us.

I was apprehensive, wondering if Greg would recognise me from earlier that morning. When they arrived, Billy looked intense, on tenterhooks, shifting his weight from side to side. He made brief introductions and then asked Greg to prophesy over us. Greg looked reluctant and turned Billy aside, saying something quietly in his ear. I wondered what it was Greg knew he didn't want to tell us.

"Don't worry," Billy said as he turned Greg back to us, his hand on his back. "They can handle it."

I wasn't so sure, however, there was no way I wanted to leave that function without hearing what he had to say. Greg clasped his hands together as if in preparation, then walked forward and, using his index finger, drew a big circle in front of us.

"There's a target right here," he said as he came to the end of the circuit. He poked his finger into the middle of the imaginary circle he'd drawn. "And the enemy is prowling around." He clarified what he'd said and then turned to Steve.

"There's a fragility about you, more you need to deal with as a man. You haven't gone deep enough yet." Then he turned his attention to me.

I felt I'd been the reason he hadn't wanted to prophesy over us, and now I was frightened of what he might say. He held my eyes hard, like he'd done earlier in the day, and I could see he was having to work himself up to bring the word.

"I'm concerned about you," he said. I figured that was a nice way of saying he thought I was dangerous. Then he mentioned something about trust, though I couldn't quite take it in. I was too busy going over his comment about his concern. "You are going to need good friends around you," he said, before addressing us as a couple again, telling us we needed to be on our guard, prayerful, and maintain good communication. Then he looked at Billy and they headed for the door.

Before we flew back to New Zealand, we popped in to see Billy in his hotel room.

"What'd you make of the prophecy from Greg?" he said.

He was sitting at the dining table with his laptop in front of him. He hadn't looked up from the screen when he'd spoken. Steve and I were sitting at the table with him, and we turned to each other as if we both thought the other should answer. I'd been in this position with Billy before, where he'd asked what I thought, but really, it was just his way of introducing the subject so he could tell you what he thought. I short-circuited the process.

"Why? What'd you think?" A smile danced from his eyes to his lips, and I wondered whether it pleased him he could get straight to the point, or rather he'd recognised my thought process and appreciated it.

"I think you guys made yourselves a target when you stood up to some people in your line of sponsorship, and you should have done that, but it's brought you into the line of fire."

I looked at Steve for confirmation and then back at Billy. I wasn't sure it was anything to do with the business; us being in the line of fire. I felt it was more to do with our relationship with him and his wife. Billy and Pauline ran a business that was bringing large numbers of people into a relationship with the Lord, and we were close to them, in a position to have an impact. That made more sense to me, though I didn't want to say that to Billy.

"It feels like we're nothing in the business though, like we wouldn't be worth worrying about," I said. Steve was quiet. Billy looked at me, clearly compiling an answer, then he looked back at his computer.

"Yeah, maybe," he said.

I didn't think he meant that. I think he thought he was right.

"I think the means of attack on you two will relate to the problem you have with men," he said looking at me.

Now that was something I could agree with him on. I quickly glanced at Steve. He was playing with the salt on the table, tipping it out and then moving it into patterns with his finger.

"I think, Steve," Billy said, trying to get his attention, "you need to protect Simone more."

I wish he hadn't said that. Greg had been right. Steve was fragile, particularly in his relationship to God and how that related to his relationship with me, but where he was confident was in his ability to protect me.

"You mean spiritually?" I said, then I cringed inwardly, knowing I'd been too quick with my comment. Billy didn't answer, and Steve looked up at both of us and then back at the salt. I could tell he was gearing up to speak.

"I think that maybe we're a target because of our relationship with you," he said. Billy moved in his seat, visibly relaxing now that Steve had entered the conversation. He took his time answering, like he was mulling things over.

"That's a worry then, isn't it?" he said, screwing his face into a grimace.

I didn't understand what he meant by that, but as if some aspect of me could make it out, my mind went back to a moment I'd witnessed in the auditorium at a function a few months earlier. It'd been during a short break in proceedings. I'd stayed in my seat, but many others were up and about. I'd seen a woman sitting on the edge of the stage on her own and I saw Billy off to the side in the wings, but he came out and headed straight for her. I remember noticing Billy's attitude when he walked up to her, like he was respectful, but it was a challenge. It made no sense to me.

She seemed a little enamoured of him, but the more she displayed that, the more guarded he seemed to become. I had understood none of it until later when I heard that the woman was married to a man in the business, but having an affair with another man, who was also in the business.

Somehow my recollection of that moment, Billy's comments about the prophecy and Steve's attitude, were all coming together to form an impression. It was all melting together in a pot and making a statement to me about who I was. It was telling me I was flawed. Damaged goods. Dangerous, just like that woman. I felt helpless; like there wasn't anything I could do to change who I'd become. And I knew how much energy it was taking to keep it under control. Giving up looked like a viable option. Just give up and go away from Steve and these people. Then nobody'd get hurt.

Steve abandoned the salt and leant back in his seat, obviously preparing to leave.

"When's your flight?" Billy said, picking up on the cue. Steve told him as he pushed up from the table. I don't think I'd ever felt relieved leaving Billy's presence before. He seemed tired now, as if being unable to impact us the way he'd wanted had wearied him. He got up from the table and hugged us warmly.

"See you back at home then," he said.

We said our goodbyes and Steve held the door open for me. I looked back just as the door closed behind us and saw Billy sitting in front of his computer again, staring off into the distance.

Led Astray

We'd been back from Australia a couple of weeks when Billy's health came to the fore. He was in hospital with heart issues. They'd been threatening for several months, with him going in and out of hospital, and because of the uncertainty, Pauline was unsure of their future on several levels. She sat on the bed in the main bedroom, her cheeks pulled in and brow knotted. I felt the need to say something reassuring, but anything I thought of sounded hollow. So instead, we talked about the things she'd take into Billy later that evening.

As we talked, a thought kept popping into my head, bothering me. I turned it aside a few times, but it was insistent. I wrestled with it to the point whereby I shifted uncomfortably on the bed, which disturbed Pauline, and she turned to me. I took it as an invitation.

"Pauline ...," I said, eyes down, unable to meet her gaze, "ya' know ... you need to watch out for me."

I hadn't liked the thought, had just wanted it removed, so I felt some release at having spent what'd built up inside. However, now I had to worry about its impact on Pauline. I don't know how she was supposed to react as I'd just told her she couldn't trust me, like I was two people and the one sitting beside her was warning her about the one in the future. I didn't feel ridiculous, as if doing that made complete sense. The funny thing is she didn't question me, just made some comment about getting on with things and got up and left the room.

Several days later, I left our son with Steve so I could grocery shop in peace. As I drove to the supermarket, I had a *Casting Crowns* CD playing, and the artist was singing about falling or sinning being a slow fade. It was the title of the song. It warned that the journey from thought to action was shorter than you might think.

As I passed the golf course, the song reached the third verse, with the artist singing about broken hearts being led astray. At that very moment, a car with the number plate 'ASTRAY' drove past. The coincidence was too strong to ignore because all morning I'd felt there was something I needed to do, that it involved Billy and Pauline, and that I was required to make it happen. I'd asked the Lord whether I was being led by the Spirit or driven by the enemy, and at the sight of the number plate, I concluded God was telling me the source of the drive was not Him. On reaching that conclusion, the drive seemed to subside. Yet, like an automaton, I mindlessly drove straight over to Billy and Pauline's.

When I got there Pauline seemed less than pleased to see me, and the reason for that escaped me, like I'd forgotten the warning I'd given her during our conversation a few days earlier. Billy was home from the hospital now, and he seemed sheepish, smiling a little too much, like he was trying to smooth over the tension in the room. He asked after Steve and our son.

"They're good—but how're you doing? What's the doctor said?"

It's funny when things get uncomfortable, how we resort to more formal ways of being together, as if structure brings a measure of control. Billy explained what the doctor had said, and whilst he did Pauline got up from the table, picked up something off the bench and left the room. When Billy had finished telling me his prognosis, he suggested we all go for lunch.

"Come on—ring Steve," he said. I must have looked unsure. "Come on—it'll do us all good."

Steve met us in a local restaurant, one that Billy and Pauline frequented. Billy was jovial with the wait staff and generous with his family and us. The staff couldn't do enough for him, and he'd been right. Lunch was fun, and Pauline relaxed. We laughed and bantered, Billy teased and cajoled, and things seemed good again. Then when it came time to go, as we headed for the cashier, there was some discussion about who should go in what car. I'd left mine at the end of Billy and Pauline's driveway so sensibly, because our son was getting scratchy, Steve took him home, and I piled into the Previa with Billy, Pauline, and the kids.

Pauline was driving, and she dropped me to my car and then rolled up to the house to let Billy out. At the restaurant she'd told us she was in a hurry, that she'd be doing a drop and run, heading somewhere with the kids. We'd arranged for Billy to get into the house using my key. However, rather than race off as we'd planned, Pauline waited while I drove up to the house, got out, and unlocked the back door for Billy. Only when I was walking back to my car did she drive off.

I started the engine and was about to drive away when, like a ground controller on the tarmac at the airport, Billy waved his arms at me. I cringed, like I could feel what was coming, and waited while he walked to the car. He moved slowly because of his size and the fact he'd just come out of the hospital. I wound down the window and when he reached the car he leant in, puffing.

"I need your keys again—the door's double locked."

"Ah," I said, turning the engine off so I could hand him my keys, "of course."

Billy returned to the back door, wending his way through the bikes and toys that littered the carport, every step looking to be a monumental effort. As I waited, I noticed the drive I'd felt earlier in the day had returned. It was a billowing presence, a pressure from within, again telling me there was something I needed to do.

I don't know whether Billy reduced his speed, or my mind slowed down what I was looking at, but a battle began, a movie clip played, of me getting out of the car, walking up behind him, arriving beside him just as he opened the door, and following him in. It was just an excerpt; I couldn't see anything beyond it, but I felt uneasy, the short clip seeming to hold some appeal. I couldn't see the logic in that as I didn't find Billy attractive, didn't want to be with him in that way, but I knew that was what the movie was intimating, tapping into something beyond what I was conscious of.

He'd reached the door, but I couldn't see what he was doing as he was in the carport's shadow. My sense of being driven shifted, no longer just a pressure but something more akin to a black panther moving stealthily through acrid air, power enhanced, up rated, and now capable of physically moving me. In the past, this force had pushed and cajoled, manipulated, and I'd responded without fully comprehending why I'd been doing what I was doing, but this was different. This time I was no longer a hapless participant, more it felt like I was being pushed against my will.

Fear coursed through me, firing down my limbs like a sharp pain. I'd spent my life taking control, had found it was the only way to feel safe. In part, that had been why riding horses had felt so good. I would manage half a ton of horse with only a bit in its mouth and some hard-earned knowledge of how to use my hands, legs, and body position to get what I wanted. That had felt a lot safer than this.

Billy turned to look at me from the doorway, like he knew something was going on. I gripped the steering wheel as if my ability to hang onto it was the difference between life and death. In some ways it was, because the force was demanding I get out of the car, and though I hated myself for it, I knew part of me wanted to. I could almost taste the power it offered. I switched my thinking to autopilot, where the only thing I let myself focus on was gripping the steering wheel. And as the thoughts entered my head, telling me what I could do, how I could take the power I wanted, I kept telling myself to grip the steering wheel. *Grip the steering wheel!*

Billy turned and came back down the steps, heading towards the car. I let my gaze move from the steering wheel to his eyes. His speed never altered, his eyes holding mine till he reached the driver's side window. I released my hand from the steering wheel, held it out and Billy dropped the keys into it, then banged on the roof twice. I only allowed myself to think of the next step. Key in the ignition and turn it, put the car in drive, and move off.

I'd not driven two minutes down the road when the phone rang. I did the sensible thing and pulled over to pick up the call. The person on the other end of the line didn't even greet me.

"Where are you?"

It was Pauline.

Out of the Swamp

2006-2008

Beth's "6 weeks, 6 months, 2 years—you choose" played on repeat in my mind, challenging me. It felt like too much weight to hold, that the pace of my healing was completely up to me. I wondered how I was supposed to think or act at a level higher than I was at. Of course, I preferred the shortest time frame, and since Beth had taught that freedom required starving my problematic ways of being with people, my response was to take a back seat in life and say no to all the things I'd normally take on. I stopped helping with events or even attending them, stopped going to meetings, stayed out of email or text exchanges and rarely went out for lunch or a coffee. It wasn't just in relation to Paul. I could see my life was a labyrinth of ulterior motives. Much of what I did served my obsessions, so I turned everything down, though I'm not sure that was what Beth had in mind. Her focus seemed to be the condition of my heart.

"You need to renew your way of thinking, how you interact with people," she said. "See yourself the way God sees you and learn to look at life and others from His heart, His perspective and not out of your own needs. This is going to take time. It's hard work, but you're up for it."

She also encouraged me to find a counsellor, and though she didn't say so, I suspected it was to replace her.

She rang one day at a pre-arranged time, for a conversation which had been a long time coming. It seemed I was low on her list of priorities, largely because I'd strongly connected in the church now. Before the call, I'd jotted down the things on my mind, and we went down the list. We discussed my excitement at the prophetic experiences I'd been having, that I was hearing God, having dreams, and seeing things move in relation to prayer, yet also, that I was still battling in my relationship with Paul. However, the conversation felt empty, like Beth was just going through the motions, and the lack of connection made me reticent to talk about the most important thing on my list. Eventually, though, I knew I had to speak or wait another couple of weeks before connecting with her again.

"Beth, I feel like our relationship has been about you discipling me."

She was slow to respond, which wasn't lost on me, and when she answered, it wasn't what I expected.

"I prefer to think of what I've been doing as mentoring," she said. Then she took a breath, perhaps purposefully leaving a gap for me to comment, but when I didn't, she went on. "God was shining His light on a particular area of your life. He wanted to highlight some truths, and I was there to challenge you in those areas, to call you back to reality."

It felt like a slap. Clearly, I still wanted more from the relationship than she wanted to give.

"Well, I've really appreciated what you've done for me," I said, trying to regain some composure. It was a good cover; I don't think she noticed how I'd withered at her interpretation of our relationship status.

"Well, it's been a privilege to walk alongside you through what the Holy Spirit has been working on," she said, and hurriedly bade me goodbye before hanging up.

My phone hand went limp. It was obvious she didn't feel the Holy Spirit's leading in our relationship anymore. It made sense of the vision I'd had a week earlier, of a butterfly alighting on a leaf and sitting there for a moment, gently batting its wings before flying off. I knew the vision was about her because her (real) name means butterfly. She'd briefly brought her wisdom and beauty into my life, and now she was gone.

With Beth bowing out, I did the only thing I could and pressed into the work with my counsellor, and as she came to understand my situation, she promoted my expansion. She encouraged my burgeoning interest in all things psychological by supporting my attendance at a counselling course in the South Island, and, under her tutelage, I tentatively became less restricted in my interactions with people at church. So, with my newfound confidence, I brought up the subject of reengaging in church projects, and she didn't hesitate.

"You're on track Simone," she said, then laughed, I think because of the look on my face. "You're so very okay. Jump right in, do all you feel to do. Don't hold back."

I had to check in with myself, make sure I hadn't drawn her into my web, manipulated her into believing I was more solid than I was, but I had to admit I felt more trustworthy. There was little to suggest I was hiding things from myself anymore, and because of that, I'd relaxed. Being around Paul was no longer a big deal; I was more genuine in the relationship, and the improvement was across the board. I was more secure in all my relationships. It was gratifying to find my growth was being enhanced by pushing in to community, rather than in keeping my distance, which was obviously something I couldn't maintain.

I joined a movement attached to the church, which focused on training young people to reach out to their peers. The young leaders welcomed my attention to detail, and the work was my bliss, administrative and relational in equal part. My involvement led to spending time with Geoff, a man people believed had quite the pastoral gift. He was a counsellor and had been a member of the church years earlier, and recently returned following a few years working in Wellington. So, though he was new to me, he was good friends with many other church members, and that made me comfortable with him from the get-go.

One glorious summer afternoon, a trailer load of equipment arrived at the church, and Geoff and I, along with a group of the youth, had the job of unloading it. Admittedly, I was not in the best headspace, feeling a little like Rachel Hunter in the Tip-Top Trumpet ad, enjoying the breeze catching my hair and the sun burning through my tee. As Geoff arrived back at the trailer to pick up another load, I lifted a heavy item and lugged it towards the door.

"Good to see you getting physically involved," he said. "It's great the youth have you to show them how to work." I laughed but took note he seemed to make a special effort.

We worked for some time, hot and sticky as it was, till the young people decided it was time for a trip to the store for hot chips and cold drinks, leaving Geoff and me with just a few more loads to take into the church. When we'd finished, the others hadn't returned, so we perched on the wheel arch of the trailer and Geoff continued with his compliments.

"Ya' know, as soon as I looked into your eyes, I knew you were a woman of God. You have this grace about you."

I was aware I needed to be wary of his appreciation, knew I was susceptible to it, but it was a balmy day, and I was feeling good, so I smiled, noticing the warmth that passed between us as I did. Fortunately, I could see the youth returning along the footpath just beyond the church and as they crossed the road we got up and walked towards them, brushing the dust from our clothes and, though nobody would have seen, as Geoff passed behind me, he gave my backside a pat.

I hadn't expected that. I knew it was deliberate, but I wasn't sure if it was a friendly gesture or something more calculating. I wasn't comfortable with it. He was married, in church leadership, I was married, and until that point had thought we were new friends getting on well and enjoying each other's company. Now I had to wonder about his intentions, worry about whether I'd given him license for the butt pat or beyond. I glanced at him as he walked past me, but he was busy greeting the youth, striking up a banter about the amount of food they'd bought.

While this situation developed, Paul was still taking up too much space in my thinking, though for an entirely different reason. I felt pained about him. He was acting strangely, ringing me seemingly for nothing at all, like he needed reassurance, and he was texting a lot. It made me aware of what a transactional relationship we'd had. I'd taken from him, and now it felt like he was taking from me, as if it were a trade. Was it to be the same with Geoff, encouraging me, and then wanting something in return?

I wrote in my journal about my sense of victory at no longer needing to control Paul, that the obsession seemed to have dissipated, yet now I was having to deal with his sudden neediness.

I felt that meant I had to work hard to hold the ground I'd taken, that the change in his behaviour was complicating things for me, but I also wanted to celebrate my victory over the obsession. But perhaps that thought was a little premature.

It seemed God wanted to speak into the situation as I had a dream. It starred the New Zealand equestrian, Mark Todd, riding in a horse trial. He'd finished the cross country and needed to get back to the showgrounds which, bizarrely, were twelve miles away. He set off at a gallop which, of course, is ridiculous. As he sped along, I was above him with a bird's-eye view, and he came across a swamp. However, rather than go around it, which I believed was an available option, he galloped through. The water was deeper than expected and Mark and his very famous bay (brown) gelding Charisma went into the sludge right up to the horse's shoulder. They struggled and Mark could get out, but Charisma battled for a long time and when the horse did eventually make it to solid ground, he'd changed colour. Now he was white.

At the time of this dream, Mark Todd had been competing on a grey (white) horse called Gandalf, so to me, the symbolism was strong; the horse going in the swamp coloured brown, struggling, and coming out the other side white. Going in as Charisma, man-made power, and coming out as Gandalf, wise, with spiritual powers of light and fire. I really wanted to know what the dream meant in my life, given it had come hot on the heels of me seeking to celebrate the change in my relationship with Paul. Was it an affirmation of my progress, or a warning?

The next few months, I went through a time of receiving what God was revealing. I wrestled with the dream, focused in on what I believed was its most important point, that it hadn't been necessary to ride through the swamp, that the choice to do so was deliberate.

I also realised that though I'd seen the rider as Mark Todd, that had only been to reveal the identity of the horses. Really, the rider was me. I'd been the one who deliberately rode through the swamp, and that was okay with God, but He was showing me what He wanted to do with what I'd chosen. He wanted me to struggle in the swamp and come out of it white, cleansed, pure as snow.

At the time I read in the study guide of my bible that though Saul, the first God appointed king of Israel, was called by God, "he struggled constantly with jealousy, insecurity, arrogance, impulsiveness, and deceit." He couldn't "wholeheartedly" trust God, "wouldn't let God's love give rest to his heart, [so] he never became God's man" (Zondervan, 2000). I'd always taken note that King David, who followed Saul as king, also had serious character flaws. He'd committed adultery, and conspired to murder to name his worst actions, but when he'd had them highlighted to him, he'd turned back to God. Interestingly God praised King David as "a man after His own heart" (1Samuel 13:14). But Saul seemed to double down on his mistakes. He couldn't trust God as David did. It was as if he never believed God had good intentions towards him.

Sunday's message at church that week, Paul taught on what Jesus had said about the kingdom of God being at hand, and that it was time to "repent and believe in the gospel"(Mark 1:15). Paul explained that to believe meant being persuaded, trusting. The way I saw it, Jesus was saying, turn from your ways and walk in Mine, trust Me. It was exactly what I believed I was being called to, the cleansing that God was after in me, the whiteness of the horse. For me to be pure as snow. It was what King David had done, turning back to God, trusting in His goodness, and what Saul had failed to do.

Then, while I was away at our church's ladies' weekend, during a time with God, I felt I was being cleansed with the word, burned from the inside out. It confirmed another prophecy I'd received a couple of years earlier, which had described me as a burning orb, the exterior crusty, with fissures through which you could see the molten fire inside. And during the weekend, a lady shared a scripture she'd received for me, about Jesus giving Himself for the church, so He might sanctify and cleanse her (the church) by washing her with the word. The purpose of washing her was so He could present her to Himself, glorious, holy, and unblemished (Ephesians 5:25-27). Again, by highlighting this for me, God was pointing to my need to be cleansed, telling me what He wanted to do so I was aware and able to get into the work with Him.

Then came what I think was the purpose of God's message to me about cleansing. I attended a prophetic conference at the end of June. I didn't receive a prophetic word throughout the event, but when it had finished, a man came and asked if he could speak to me. I was a little taken aback. I didn't know who he was, but I followed him to a seat. He told me:

> You think you're a mouse, but you're going to roar. Don't worry about what you're going to say. He has built wisdom into you. There are bellows blowing you up. You need to be around those who fan the flames. Anatomically, you don't know where you fit, but you're perfectly made for the place He has for you.

It was powerful as a stand-alone word, but in early July came the clincher, the second or third witness (Deuteronomy 19:15).

I was on the worship team during a service. I believe we were mid-song when a young woman who had a strong prophetic gift walked from the back of the auditorium and stood in front of us. One of my fellow singers elbowed me to let me know I was the one the young woman was addressing. She called out:

> You think you're weak, but you're strong, you think you're a mouse but you're a lion, and you're going to roar.

God and Me

2009-2010

5:12pm, 21st July, "Death is swift." The words came powerfully and directly, like I'd heard them audibly. I wrote them down, including the exact time. I've never received a word that same way since. I asked God to trust me with more; to speak about it to my heart, but I heard nothing till a week later. Had I known what was coming, I might have preferred not to hear it.

Beth had a life-threatening illness. I would have appeared okay about it, but I wasn't. In my journal, I spoke to God, asking Him what was going on in me, told Him I was hurting, that I recognised it as pain, but I couldn't figure out the source. It was as if I didn't understand it, a disconnect between the pain and the emotion that was producing it. Then, hot on the heels of the pain, came anger. I'd been thinking a lot about Beth's situation, and what God would want me to do and become within it. I said to Him I wanted to be genuine in thanking Him for what He was doing in her life, wanted to know His will so I could work in it with Him. Of course, logically I thought the pain was grief, but I told Him I seemed to have no ability to manage it, nowhere inside me to file it. The anger made no sense.

It was perhaps the first time I'd recognised that an emotion I was responding with wasn't really the one I'd have expected. I should have been sad, in fact on some level I was, but the emotion coming to the fore was anger. Of course, I was frightened she might die, but the anger was confusing. Then I received an email from Beth, which made me painfully aware it might be the last one I ever got. I realised my fear for her was more a fear for me, that I wouldn't be okay if she were no longer in my life. So, another layer of control was under threat. That was why I was angry.

In a separate conversation, God was also talking about the troubling things I see in people, things that maybe they can't see which are causing them strife, that I was to overlook them unless He wanted me to address them. I wasn't to repeat them, to dwell on them, or compare myself to them—only overlook them. He went further, talking to me about the words we speak about each other. If those words don't bring life, if they're gossip, it inhibits His ability to bless us.

On Sunday, during worship, I felt led to lie face down at the back of the auditorium in complete, worshipful submission. Then, at the end of the service, there was a call forward for prayer.

"Come, even if you're not sure you're meant to," the speaker said.

I knew that comment was for me. I'd been wrestling with whether I should go forward, wondering if I was just attention seeking, something I still felt I needed to check in with myself about.

Two of the church's leading prayer warriors ministered to me, and I slid to the ground, my mouth tingling. I hadn't been down long when I looked up and my gaze settled on an elder. He asked if I wanted him to pray for me and I nodded, then sat on the pew beside him.

"What do you want prayer for?" he said.

"My mouth."

"Why? What's wrong with it?"

I laughed. "Nothing. It's what comes out of it."

He knew exactly what to do, speaking to me about the moment Isaiah sees the Lord in all His glory, and he's undone. Then the seraph takes a live coal from the altar and touches Isaiah's mouth with it, saying, "Behold, this has touched your lips; and your iniquity is taken away and your sin is forgiven" (Isaiah 6:7). It drew together all the indicators I'd received about needing to get in the cleansing process with God and His conversation with me about the words I speak, that it was part of the cleansing I was to go through. The elder prayed that the words I spoke would be anointed and wise, and I'd overcome the temptation to speak contrary to the Spirit.

I thought that was the end, but at home after falling asleep for an hour or so, a nana nap, I awoke with the word Ahithophel on my mind. I thought maybe the speaker had mentioned it that morning, but I checked my notes, and no. I searched it up and found it was the name of King David's counsellor. So, all of it, the prophetic words, the dreams, my conversations with God, seemed to point to me going through a cleansing process and then being commissioned as a counsellor or speaker in some capacity.

Then came another dream. This time I saw a horse in a paddock, distressed, galloping up and down, wheeling around and kicking out. It caught a leg in the fence and reared up, tearing the wire off the posts. I tried to help, but part of the fence flicked up and landed in a noose around my neck. I knew any second the horse could bolt and pull the noose tight, so I called out to my father to bring the wire cutters. I got the noose from around my neck, but then it caught around my head. My father was coming, but he was walking slowly, like he couldn't see the danger I was in. I yelled at him to cut the wire and the dream ended.

My understanding at the time was simplistic. The dream matched a recurring one I'd had as a child, our house on fire, dad leaving the house with me on his shoulders, but me falling backwards off his shoulders and him failing to notice. I knew it had something to do with my dad's inability to be there for me, but in time I came to realise there was far more depth to it than that. However, at this point I couldn't fully understand what was being told to me, but I could respond spiritually, so I prayed:

> Lord, teach me what to focus on. I know this is not about my relationship with my dad, it's about You and me ...

Dam Busting

I pulled on the handle, and the resistance, the clatter of the old spindle reminded me of the door to the home my family had lived in during the seventies. The sense was appropriate, the handle undoubtedly original, and the old brick and tile that housed the chiropractic clinic had lived way beyond its heyday. The rooms were now painted in modern greys and whites, but the building still clung to the boxy layout that defined its original time and place.

Singsong tones greeted me from behind the counter, and Sue, the receptionist picked up my file and made to walk down the hallway.

"You can go straight through if you like. Tina's just finishing up with a new client." I raised the edges of my mouth in a weak smile, took the file, saving her the trouble of leading the way, and headed down the hall.

There were three tables to choose from, but I always took the one by the window. It was older and more comfortable, probably from years of use. There was background music playing, most likely Spanish guitar, and the scent of an essential oil burning on the desk. I took my shoes off and lay down, face pressed into the hole at the top of the table. There was something pleasurable about the sensation that ran through me then, like the act had released a hold, and I sometimes wondered whether that was all the adjustment I needed.

I breathed the way I'd been taught, drawing breath into my lower body and gradually rolling it through my torso, my body undulating with the wave of air. It was difficult getting the breath to my skull. It was stalling between my shoulder blades where I'd been experiencing pain all morning, a physical manifestation of the angst I was feeling.

My mind was the proverbial record stuck in a crack, reminding me of the conversation I'd had with Paul the previous day. I'd worried about a chastising email I'd sent one of the youth leaders, thinking I may have been out of line, and because I'd copied Paul in on the original, I sent a text asking him if we could catch up about it. He'd come straight back saying, if possible, he'd like to talk about it right then. I'd felt a rush at his instant reply, a residue of the sense of power and control I'd felt in the past when he'd responded quickly. I'd rung him, and we'd talked for an hour and a half, though not so much about the situation with the youth leader. The conversation had been heartening because of its content. We'd often had long discussions about the church, books, or about his or my relationships with different people, but this time we talked about how we related to each other, and what that meant. I felt he'd been curious about me, not just what I thought about the things that involved him or the church, yet as the conversation had naturally drawn to a close it was obvious the depth of it had affected him, and he seemed to arrive at some sort of epiphany.

"I think I've withheld myself in our relationship," he said.

For him to admit he'd not been able to give himself fully wasn't a surprise. In fact, I'd have thought him foolish if he hadn't maintained a level of reserve.

"Perhaps that was appropriate," I said.

I then spent the afternoon basking in the aftermath of our conversation, rejoicing, feeling a sense of richness in that I felt more known by him than I had before. However, as evening came, his "I think I've withheld myself in our relationship" echoed in me like a clanging bell, causing me to query what he'd meant. Poised at the back of my mind was a line of thought, which seemed to have been loitering, waiting for the right circumstance to present itself. Paul had found me attractive from the outset. That was the gist of it, something I'd always thought possible but had never really believed. If it were true, it meant the struggle I'd been involved in wasn't one sided, that he could carry some of the blame. Then again, if he found me attractive, it threw considerable doubt on aspects of our relationship that I treasured. The joy and enthusiasm he occasionally displayed when we spent time together, or his absolute delight when I'd played the violin during worship one time, a response you'd expect from a father. And what of my feelings of worth after our conversation that day? Did his pleasurable responses mean something other than I was a joy to be with?

And not content with that line of thought, I ratcheted up the tension further by wondering, if Paul had found me attractive, whether he'd ever had any intention of acting on it. Which had led to the most confronting question of all. How would I have responded? I'd wrestled all night with that one, and the stress and subsequent pain in my neck and shoulder was the reason for my visit to the chiropractor that morning.

Eventually Tina breezed into the room and though I couldn't see her because I was face down on the table, I knew her chocolate fondue eyes would be glowing. Straight away, she began asking questions, checking in like she always did. I batted her questions back, just enough of an answer to be polite and eventually she realised she was doing all the work in the conversation and shifted course, just telling me the areas she wanted me to get breath to as she made the adjustments.

Her practice worked with the body's natural repair process, so sometimes it seemed she could read my mind by what she understood of the responses in my body. When she had me flip onto my back and breathe into the centre of my breastbone, it reminded me of a conversation we'd had only a month or two earlier, about the purpose of pain in the body. She'd said it was evidence of a build-up of tension, a warning of a blockage. The pain let you know you needed to get rid of it, to cause the body to release it, and her job was to help me do that. She'd explained it that day as a dam which needed busting, to enable the flow of healing to get through to all the starved areas. She touched the centre of my breastbone and told me to breathe into it. It was easier now as following her adjustments, the breath flowed more freely.

With the fresh flow came a new question, one that had been lurking in the dark recesses of my mind. If I'd known Paul was holding himself back, would I have pressed him, pushed for a response during the times I'd sensed his vulnerability? I never had, even when my need was at its greatest, always so certain the issues were mine alone. Oh, I'd seen his enjoyment of me, but I'd seen him that way with others, and there was always a genuineness about his behaviour, which threw considerable doubt on there being any ulterior motive.

Suddenly Tina spoke, reminding me of her presence.

"Just a couple more breaths and you can get up when you're ready."

I liked I got to choose my timing, and eased myself back into a sitting position, pausing to wipe under my eyes to remove any smudged mascara. Tina was writing in my file and without looking up, made a comment, half statement, half query.

"You're wrestling with a huge existential question," she said.

I drove home smoothly; the traffic drifting silently around me. Somehow, the thinking I'd engaged in had undermined the sense of safety I'd always felt with Paul. It had occurred to me I might have been resting heavily on his goodwill all this time, on his ability to keep our relationship at an appropriate level, but now I was understanding there'd always been a fallible human being on the other end of my actions. In my search for safety, to feel protected, I'd believed I couldn't trip him up, had had a naïve faith that nothing I did would cause him to fall. Now I had to wrestle with the possibility that my faith had been in the wrong place, and I might have been walking a tightrope the entire time.

A Faithful Woman?

I couldn't speak to anyone at the church about what had happened with Geoff, couldn't risk colouring their opinion of him, especially since it was only a butt pat. He was away in the months that followed anyway, so I pushed it to the back of my mind until the next incident, which inevitably came. Perhaps by not responding, I'd given an ascent to it.

We'd gathered the youth in the church for a meeting, and when it finished, we crowded at the back of the auditorium to funnel through a single door. I knew Geoff was behind me, felt he was overly close, his proximity not really dictated by the circumstances, though he could have used it as an excuse. I felt him touch me on my hip, not a bump. He didn't brush up against me; he put his hand on me. I whipped around and stared at him, surprised he'd done something like that again, and I think my reaction shocked him.

"Your top was caught in your belt," he said, appearing sheepish. I didn't respond, but turned to face the front and carried on. Again, you could construe it as reasonable, but I felt it wasn't. I recorded the incident in my journal but kept my concern to myself.

The last straw was when he and I were sitting at a table in the café, people everywhere, so completely non-threatening, but he steered the conversation to the state of his marriage. He told me he and his wife had nothing in common and that they'd nearly split a few years back. He was watching me closely when he said it, and I looked down at the cup I was holding, trying to divest the moment of its intensity. I could feel him demanding something from me, and I didn't like it.

"Well, I'm proud of my faithfulness," I said.

I suppose I could only have meant that from the perspective of The Law rather than the way Jesus spoke of it (Matthew 5:28). Either way, I don't think it was quite the response he was expecting. In fact, I think he may have felt insulted, or judged, given I'd compared his marriage to mine, and I continued to do so.

"I believe I'm a faithful woman," I said, holding eye contact.

He recovered quickly, his next comment seemingly an attempt to slap me back, metaphorically, of course.

"You sound like you're trying to convince yourself."

I paused, checking to see if there was any truth in his observation, but quickly decided that if there was some convincing going on, it was none of his business, and there was a faith in God's strength, grace and mercy impacting the situation that he wasn't conversant with. However, I knew what he'd said might haunt me, which was perhaps his intention.

"No, but it has been a battle for me," I said, to show my statement wasn't from a position of willful blindness.

If that'd been the end of things, I don't think I would have given it much more thought. He'd done all the running, but for reasons unknown to me even now, that was about to change. Even though I had no interest in this man other than the enjoyment of someone who was fun to work alongside, it was as if I had to respond to what I considered advances, to affirm him, prop up his ego, because I liked him as a friend. What I really should have done was remind myself of what Beth had once asked me in relation to my behaviour around Paul.

"What makes you think he needs you to feel good about himself?" she'd said.

Geoff upped the ante in our relationship by giving me responsibility for an event he was normally in charge of, and publicly acknowledged I was the right person for the job, praising me at length in front of the youth. I felt special—chosen, and studiously performed, feeling all the while that the most important thing I needed to do was live up to the standard he'd set. I was zealous, to the point of being alone at church late one night, when everyone else had gone, apart from a small group of the youth talking out in the car park.

It had occurred to me that Geoff had asked me to do the job to make sure it left me alone at church so he could turn up when no one was around, so I waited. I should have been gone long ago, and if someone had found me there, it would have looked completely out of place. I was on shaky ground once again, but I kept waiting because I was so sure he'd show up, perhaps needed him to, to confirm my suspicions. I'm not sure what purpose I thought that would serve.

It got to the stage where I was more than an hour late home, with no reasonable explanation, and Geoff hadn't turned up. How mortifying. The funny thing is I still wondered whether he was around, watching to see if I'd waited for him. It was a ridiculous thought. Yet I was so sure I was right about his intentions that no other explanation seemed viable unless he was waiting for the group of youth holed up in the car park to leave, which they never did.

Eventually, I succumbed to the pressure of Steve's expectation that I'd be home, and I was glad of the drive. It gave me a chance to compose myself and deal with the realisation that maybe I'd read the situation wrong. I may have been close to proving Geoff right, that I wasn't a faithful woman at all.

I felt I'd dodged a bullet, not tested in a vulnerable moment, though if Beth had heard of my behaviour, she'd have said I hadn't gotten away with anything. I'd damaged myself. But it was a comment from the church administrator which revealed things may not have flown completely under the radar.

Des and I were chatting in the church café some two weeks later. I had a lot of respect for him, and I think the feeling was mutual. Eventually he got around to church business and asked about an item of church property mislaid when I'd been working on the project for Geoff. I didn't know where it was, so I told him I'd find out. I'd just ring Geoff. But as I began scrolling through my contacts, Des' demeanor completely changed.

"Why've you got Geoff's number?"

I recoiled. The hidden question was obvious. I had lots of numbers in my phone belonging to men in the church, Des would know that. I had Des' phone number in there. I was pretty sure he was questioning either my intentions in the relationship, or Geoff's. In fact, he'd been around the greater church community his whole life. Conceivably, he could know of the baggage Geoff might carry and be concerned about me.

However, what I most strongly remembered was my actions, and the shame flooded through me, but I knew the show had to go on. I had to convince Des I had no reason to be ashamed.

"Why wouldn't I have his number?"

He held my indignant gaze. I knew I had to win the staring contest. Otherwise, he'd believe he had valid suspicions. But who did I think I was kidding?

Foreign Wives

God was talking to me about foreign wives. It seemed to be a difficult conversation as I'd been unsettled, eating too much, and waking at four in the morning most nights. I'd read in the book of Ezra that the Israelites pledged to put away their foreign wives and I felt the intimation from God was, so should I. From what I'd read in scripture, a foreign wife represented finding security in something outside of God. Certainly, the evidence in my life was clear. When I wasn't concentrating on Him, my heart raced off after other people.

At church on Sunday, Paul was his normal, friendly self, and in the face of that I was calm, the obsession with him appearing now to be past tense. I asked God if that was a foreign wife I'd put away, but I didn't receive any confirmation. During the service, Paul preached on change, that it's choosing for the better, and that when Jesus comes again, He will punish the spiritually stagnant (Zephaniah 1:12). Paul said the antidote was to walk with the wise, to love discipline, and to "Let the righteous smite me in kindness and reprove me; It is oil upon the head; Do not let my head refuse it ..." (Psalm 141:5). He told us to pray about the change we wanted for the year. I immediately thought of the foreign wives' conversation with God, particularly in relation to the project I'd carried out for Geoff, how I'd been tempted and put myself in an unsafe position.

A couple of months later, I crossed paths again with the prophet Greg Burson. He came to our church and picked me out of the crowd, delivering the following word:

> Not everything that happens ... in life is exactly the way we would have played the hand if we'd had the chance to organise things. Some things have come at you, and you have probably thought, well, "why me?" And it's because I think God has always been the one who shapes your providence. He's the one who knows the grace that you need and the grace that you have. Tell your story. Tell people what you have coped with and carried, what you have worked through, and what you have walked through. Let that unfold in front of people and watch them be amazed at the goodness of God in a person's life. Providence is a wonderful thing, and God's providence has always been a big part of how life has gone for you. Remember the word providence. It's kind of like Romans 8:28. He works everything together for good in a way that only He can understand, and I just hope that He puts you more and more in the picture, because the story that you will write and the words that you write down will become a testimony and a story that others will read. Habakkuk was an amazing prophet who had a complaint in his heart and God said write the complaint down so that people can run with it. Cos ... your deep complaint is your vision, and it's your story and you write it down and you watch how people will run with it.

After the meeting, Greg took me aside and told me that while he'd been speaking to me, the song "Money, Money, Money" had been playing in his head. I was interested that he'd heard an Abba song, as they were the first music group I'd listened to when I was young. I went home and listened to it again, gleaning it was about going out and getting what you want because it's your security, a plan to get supposed heaven on earth for yourself. A foreign wife, if you will.

Weeks later, Tony Saxon, another prophet, also came to our church and again I was picked out of the crowd. He told me:

This is a name changing season for you. There's this piece in the Old Testament where He talks about them no longer calling what is precious worthless. I felt the Lord saying I am changing so much about who you are that you will define things differently in yourself, you will define things differently in your past, you will define things differently in your current situations because God has and will continue to refashion your mind so that your words have power to them, so that when you speak to people, you will be able to say to them, in comfort and in truth, "this is not worthless, this is precious." And God has not only given you a gift of compassion but will allow you to outwork compassion and mercy in people's lives. People will hope again because you intervened with them, people will believe again because you said it's okay, people will pray again because you have brought them back to a place of prayer. It's almost like God has given you a gift of evangelising people who are the prodigals really, the people who have strayed in their hearts, not necessarily from church but people who have come out of that place of intimacy with God. I felt like the Lord said, you will feel it on them, you will be able to redefine it to them and speak it differently to them, so it's almost like changing the way they see things, changing their names, and really speaking hope and life into them.

Both prophecies confirmed things I'd had on my mind for a while. I'd journaled for years and had always sensed I'd eventually write something using what I'd recorded. And the books I liked to read fed my interest in understanding the problematic ways people engage with the world. Both words showed the direction I would take in the years to come, but Tony Saxon's words also spoke about what was to occur in the coming months.

Following the chill of winter's arrival, a coldness emerged in the church. It was dense, like a gel, difficult to move through and, as if we were all determined to have our own way, the church divided. Without really understanding why, I prayed. The way I described it in my journal was I "complained" about being unable to have the relationship with Paul I wanted. There was no precursor, not one I was consciously aware of. I couldn't put my finger on exactly why now I felt like praying for something better. In fact, it seemed out of place. I'd never specifically spoken to God about the relationship, being reticent in asking for anything in relation to Paul beyond help with my issues.

I couldn't even explain what kind of relationship I wanted, though I knew I didn't want that wary, distancing people fall into. How they keep everything at a safe level by not dealing with what's lacking in their relationship with the Lord, which is often the very thing that's making them unsafe. They settle for limping through life, not receiving all there is to be gained from the relationships God might have providentially provided. But now I needed to ask God for what I wanted. And like the child who suddenly realises their parents know best, I was open and willing for God to do His will. So, my prayer was childlike, without guile.

"Father, I want a relationship with Paul that is of You."

And wouldn't you know it? The next thing, the church leadership fired Paul. It seemed disconnected; it wasn't. Not that I thought they fired him because of my prayer. But the complaining about my relationship with Paul, and the sudden alteration of his position in my life, that was, as Tony Saxon had prophesied, a part of the redefining process I was to go through.

Days later, Geoff rang me, which wasn't something he normally did. After the uncomfortable incidents, I'd kept my distance, so it'd been a while since I'd spoken to him. I was back at my mother's place for a holiday weekend with my son.

"I hear there's been a few changes at the church," Geoff said. He'd left a few weeks earlier to take up a short-term counselling role down country, so obviously someone from the church had been in touch with him.

Mum, Elijah and I had just walked into the local gentlemen's club, which, unusually, yet somewhat typically for my mother, she was president of. I waved and smiled at the lady behind the bar. She was used to me coming in with my mum from time to time.

"You hear right," I said into the phone, "word must travel fast, eh?"

It was a bit of an ego boost for him to have rung me. There were many other people I'd have thought would have been more important and, with a far greater influence, who could have updated him on what was happening. I chatted a bit about my shock at the elders firing Paul with no conversation with the congregation, and we discussed the reaction to the news of one of the young leaders who Geoff and I were both close to. Then I noticed the conversation clumsily shifted back to what I intended doing about what had occurred.

"There's a forum about it on Thursday, isn't there?" Geoff said.

I agreed as I watched the lady behind the bar give Elijah a fizzy drink.

"How're you going to handle that? Are you going?" he said.

Mum pointed at a cup, and I nodded my assent to a tea as I turned back to the call.

"Well, I was gonna ring you to get your thoughts on what's happened ..."

"That's good...," he said.

"... Just to get another view on things," I said. "I'm planning to go to the meeting. There should be an opportunity to speak."

His response was slow.

"You know ... I wonder whether you should just go along ... hear what's being said, but not get involved."

"Oh, okay. Really?"

Till that moment I'd felt gung-ho about things, sure of my path through the situation, but his comment slowed me down. It checked me.

"Why shouldn't I say something?"

This time, he was quick to respond.

"You don't want to put yourself in a position you can't come back from. Better to keep yourself separate from the opinions of others."

His advice surprised me, and I could feel my internal gears graunching in response. Once I was off the call, though, I was immediately engaged in conversation with Mum and the lady behind the bar, so I didn't have time to think about things until later that evening when I was back at Mum's for the night. I'd put Elijah to bed and was sitting with my books and journal. I replayed the conversation with Geoff and as I did, the abrupt alteration in its course stood out. I realised something was wrong, that he'd had a hidden purpose in calling me.

As I followed that line of thought, I felt a fear playing in the pit of my stomach, which wound its way up my body and wrapped its tentacles around my heart. I'd misread things. I'd assumed Geoff would only think of me in our conversation about the situation at church, but now I remembered he was good friends with some of the elders. He'd known them for years. His allegiance wouldn't be with me. And then I remembered Geoff wasn't even that fond of Paul, but he knew we were close. I panicked, suddenly seeing I may have made a terrible mistake. I backtracked, rushing, trying to recall the entirety of our conversation, wondering if I'd said anything that could be harmful to Paul.

This final incident with Geoff caused me to question everything I knew about him. It was like he was not who he purported to be. I'd thought he was someone I could trust, but I realized that was based on him being friends with others in the congregation. But what if they knew who he was and made allowances for his weaknesses?

I realised I could no longer reconcile the 'butt pat', the 'shirt adjustment' or the 'faithful woman' conversation in the way I had been, and I needed to talk about it with someone. But again, I was wary, not wanting to sully Geoff's reputation unnecessarily. So, when I got back to Auckland, I told Steve. Just about the physical touches, not the 'faithful woman' conversation. I think I assumed he would ease my mind, tell me I was overreacting, that it was nothing. But his response was the complete opposite. It was like I'd played straight into a pattern of thought he was already deeply involved in, as if he'd already had reservations about Geoff. In fact, it seems likely Steve's intuition about Geoff's motives had been plaguing him for some time.

We were sitting in the lounge, the 55-inch television that dominated the room on mute, and Steve was statue-like, his eyes ice cold.

"Why have you taken so long to tell me about this?"

I wasn't sure I'd ever intended telling him. "I don't know—I just couldn't hang onto it any longer."

Steve's face was deadly. It was like an inky cloud had descended on him. "So, what did you do at the time? What did you say to him?"

I could feel myself cowering. "I didn't say or do anything. I just ignored it."

"Both times?"

"Yes."

"Did what he'd done bother you?"

Of course, it had. I'd written it in my journal and from then on, been watchful. "It surprised me, but I didn't know what to do."

Steve looked away.

I was afraid I'd created the conditions that had led to Geoff's actions. I'd been friendly, we'd had fun together. I couldn't be sure I hadn't invited the escalation in his attention, but I was loath to tell Steve that. He might question what I thought I'd done that would encourage such a response, and I didn't know what to say? I loved the camaraderie I experienced with the likes of Geoff. I didn't want to stop being that way. It felt like one of the joys of life.

Steve's attention seemed to be caught by the muted movement on the television. "I don't want you to have anything more to do with him," he said, eyes still on the screen.

It took a moment for that to settle over me, but before I could say anything, Steve continued.

"No more projects, no texts, no emails, and no phone calls," he said.

Straight away, I was thinking of the practicalities. Geoff's actions had made me feel unsafe, not completely, but certainly upon reflection. And Steve, wanting to step in, felt right. I wanted to be protected.

"But I have to say something to him, otherwise he's going to keep coming back to me. He'll want to know what's happened."

I shouldn't have worried; Steve knew exactly how to handle the situation.

"Email him one last time. Tell him no more contact, and you won't be entering any conversations about why you're cutting him off."

Steve was resolute, but he didn't need to be. He wasn't getting any argument from me. I was concerned, though, about the response from Geoff such an abrupt action on my part might elicit. I couldn't stand for there to be any sort of showdown between him and Steve. I knew the whole thing could end up making me look like a fool. There wasn't any solid evidence I could point at to say Geoff was in the wrong. People could pass it off as me reacting sensitively. I knew I didn't trust Geoff anymore, and I also had an inkling my heart in the matter might not be squeaky clean. Seeing me falter, though, Steve seemed to think it was in relation to his demands.

"Either you email him, or I will," he said.

Of course, I emailed Geoff. I told him I'd no longer be involved in any of the projects we'd worked on together, and that he needed to direct any queries or contact about them to the church office. I put a PostScript at the bottom of the email telling him this wasn't a decision I would enter any conversations about. I emailed at 6.30pm on Saturday night.

And Sunday morning at 8.30am, Geoff rang. I knew it would be him. Like the old saying goes, I was just waiting for your call. Even before I picked up the phone, I made a mental note of where Steve was—still in bed and, I hoped, still asleep. Geoff gave me no chance to collect my thoughts before launching straight into questions about my email.

"What's wrong? Your email sounded so final. You're holding some sort of offense against me, aren't you?"

I hadn't expected him to be so direct; to suggest I was upset with him.

"Don't you trust me?" he asked, his voice tight, shocking in its level of intensity.

"No" I said. I didn't trust him, and I didn't trust myself to say anything else to clarify that. He didn't speak for a moment, his turn to feel like he'd misjudged the relationship.

I was gaining confidence in my ability to turn him away. Steve was an angry husband, and I was worried about what he might be capable of if Geoff didn't get the message. Geoff continued to fire questions at me, trying to trip me up, to get me to alter my position and in return I just shut down, refusing to involve my heart. I knew all I had to do was get him off the phone with enough of a lack of reaction on my part that he would never bother to contact me again.

"I'm sure you're holding some sort of offense with me—Simone, won't you please just tell me what it is?"

"No—I'm just not going to be involved in any of the projects we've been working on anymore, and I don't want to talk about the reasons."

We went through every version of those two sides of the conversation several times before he gave up. "I feel like you're walking into a very dark cave," he said.

His comment made me suspect he felt guilty and cornered and was busy laying the groundwork to distance himself from any blame. I was pleased I'd held my ground. All the way through the conversation, I'd had to battle the part of me that wanted to tell him exactly what was going on, but my loyalty to Steve had drowned it out. Geoff attempted to garner some evidence of an emotional connection from me.

"I don't care that you don't want to be involved in anything anymore. I just can't stand for our relationship to be broken."

"And I just can't be in contact with you anymore, Geoff. I'm sorry."

"No, I'm sorry," he said. His comment hung in the air for a moment, so I ended the call.

Testing Times

2011

All roads led to counselling. I'd attended two counselling courses, had found I resonated strongly with the material, and both times the course leaders told me I had a natural aptitude and recommended I train. So, I applied to a college and was quickly called in for a group interview.

We sat in a circle in a small room; two lecturers and five potential students. I felt solid amongst them, comfortable, something of a new experience for me. The sense I had was that no matter what they threw at me, I was a match for it. My life had led me here, and all I'd walked through and worked through meant I was ready.

The lecturers introduced themselves and had us do the same, then asked us to tell stories about our lives. My confidence level meant I was happy to go first, and I told the story of the vow I'd made as a fourteen-year-old, to never ask my father to do anything with me again. I went through how his rebuff of my request to play tennis that day must have been the final straw in a life in which I felt he'd rarely been there as I thought he should. My story visibly moved the lecturers and my fellow students, and as they spoke of their experience of it, each of them seemed to consider what my response to my father might mean in their life. Other stories followed, and we all shared what we thought and felt in response, and as we left the room a couple of hours later, I was confident, based on how the interview had gone, that my acceptance into the program was sure.

The first day on campus brought evidence of the reason God wanted me there. I'd thought it was to get a qualification, but it appeared I was to gain far more than a counselling degree. At the Powhiri, the traditional Māori welcome for new students, the Kaikaranga (Māori female caller) led us into the auditorium, and we sat facing all the existing students and lecturers. It was a solemn moment, yet a man in the second row of the crowd opposite began troubling me with some prolonged eye contact. Each time I noticed him staring, he'd look away.

As the semester got into full gear, I learned this man was a lecturer, a teacher, so literally catnip for me and my issues. Yet rather than feeling flattered like I would have in the past, I found his attention frustrating. I had to deal with it, knew it was there, and had some idea of why that might be. I even felt compassion for him in what I'd learned was a difficult battle, considering I'd fought it for so long. But I felt no pride in having captured his interest. I knew it wasn't about me, in the same way my issues had never been about anyone else.

However, what I didn't notice at the time was how this incident mirrored my situation with the man on the marae all those years ago. It was only later I saw the lecturer's attention may have been a test of my heart, not for God's benefit, but for mine. In immediately picking up on the reality of the situation and responding with compassion and wisdom, I saw the evidence of the progress I'd made, and that was encouraging. But that test was not the only one I would be sitting.

With Paul fired from our church, after much deliberation I left too. It caused a lot of upheaval in my relationships, and though it wasn't ideal, I found I needed something familiar in my new college life. I found it in the company of another mature student, Pete. Though I hadn't met him before, I'd seen him at a church we'd been checking out, and somehow the familiarity and impression of solidity he embodied gave me a sense of stability in those early weeks of the semester.

We were in group together, the training ground for baby counsellors. It was where we'd wrestle with our rough edges, during the open and honest responses of others. The lecturers placed seven or eight students with two facilitators, and every week two from the group would tell a story about themselves. The rest of the group would reflect on how the story and its delivery had impacted them. It was all about experiencing the other and noticing the effect they had on you, and, conversely, your impact on them.

There was another man in our group, younger, in his late twenties, and initially, he too seemed to look for stability while he found his feet at college. In our first few weeks of training, the three of us became a bit of a sub-group, part of the greater group of about thirty-five full-time counselling students, but often flowing back together after connecting with others for a time. Not that we were closer, just there was more familiarity in our connection, like going back to the place you grew up and walking the streets you'd once ridden your Raleigh Twenty along.

I noticed the younger man watching how Pete and I related, as if we weren't quite behaving as he'd expected, not fulfilling the model he had of how a man and a woman married to other people should relate. I didn't mind his confusion. In fact, I found it funny and perhaps unfairly, sometimes teased him a little, because I was confident in where I stood and wanted to challenge his preconceptions.

The college delivered our counselling courses in blocks, two full days of lectures for each course, twice during the semester. When we got breaks in the sessions, the whole counselling crowd ended up in the main foyer, standing or sitting in groups around one of the large tables. We'd have our lattes, muffins, K-bars or pies, there'd be comers and goers in the conversations, and people talking in couples and threesomes within the larger group. There'd be joiners in from other programs, adding to the diversity of the conversation, and there'd sometimes be raucous laughter as the group singled out one or two for some gentle, collegial ribbing.

It was during one of these moments, in the corner under the stairs with a group predominantly made up of counselling students, that our young friend made his move. It was as if he couldn't hold his curiosity in any longer. I watched the thought roll across his face as he looked at me sitting two down from Pete, the usual banter going on. His brow furrowed, which served as a warning, his eyes held mine and I felt a check in my heart, a knowing that something was coming. One of our close friends, a lovely redhead, glanced at him and then me, also appearing to discern something was about to happen. There was a staggered pause in the groups' conversations, like we as a collective took a deep breath, and my young friend looked like he'd overcome his final objection.

"What's going on between you two?" he said, looking at me but glancing quickly at Pete to ensure I knew which two he was referring to.

All conversation ceased, some jaws dropped, and all eyes swung my way because although he'd said, "between you two," something about the way he'd said it seemed to lay the question squarely at my feet. I felt a surge of heat rise to my face and deliberately didn't speak for a moment, wanting his query to settle on me. The young man continued to question with his eyes, and I steadily returned his gaze.

"Does the way we get on bother you?" I asked.

His eyes held mine firmly, questioning. He had the look of one making an honest appraisal, which wasn't offensive. In fact, I was pleased he was being open by asking in front of everyone and not talking about it behind our backs.

"Whoa, what a question to ask. Is this alright with you?" someone asked me. Their question added to my sense of safety in the group, and it bolstered me.

"It's okay," I said, glancing at the speaker. Then I looked back at our young friend, who was still expectant, but a little flustered since I'd thrown the focus of his question back on him.

"No, it doesn't bother me, really. I just wonder if it's okay?"

Wow, that said a lot—not necessarily about him, maybe more about the culture of the church, the environment we all lived in.

"We're just friends," I told him. I let my eyes drop, but I hadn't finished. It was a valid question, and I felt it was important to answer fully, thinking it would be helpful to him if I explained how the relationship felt, so I went on.

"When we first started this course, I felt a bit wobbly. I'd just gone through a church division, and it had undermined my sense of place in the world. I'd seen Pete before, though we'd not met, and there was something about him that made me feel safe. I'd been through a lot of change and loss of relationships, and in this new environment I felt I needed something ... some temporary shoring up, I suppose."

My young friend looked at me hard, probably weighing up whether he thought I was in full possession of the facts, or whether I was hiding something from myself as well as everyone else. After a painfully lengthy period during which I felt the weight of the whole group's expectations, his gaze broke from mine and he smiled, mumbling something about not really understanding, but being resigned to it.

I'd explained, hoping perhaps it addressed the part of the relationship which had appeared questionable to him, but in doing so, I noticed something important. I'd felt no guilt or condemnation when he'd asked the question. The sense of guilt which previously accompanied such scrutiny, or the impression I sometimes had of being accused, I hadn't felt it this time. I understood that to mean the place I was standing was solid beneath me.

Outlier

Halfway through the first year of study, I had lunch with an old friend. We knew each other from church, which, by then, I hadn't been attending for eight months. I was feeling quite separate from the happenings on my old stamping ground which made what came next quite a shock.

We'd not long taken our seats in a cheap Vietnamese restaurant when she fixed her eyes on mine and asked the question, I believe, was the driving force behind her desire to get together.

"Of course, you know about the rumour, don't you?" she said.

I must have looked confused, so she paused, appearing torn, as if unsure whether she should continue. She looked down as she made her choice.

"It's about you, so I think you should," she said.

The way she put it felt accusatory, instantly putting me on high alert. Even more concerning, she looked dubious, appearing unsure whether I truly was ignorant of what she was about to tell me. Her behaviour made me wonder if I really wanted to know what she'd heard.

I smiled. "No—I haven't heard a rumour," I said.

She slowed the moment dramatically, suddenly enthralled with the condiments on the table, and haltingly told me she'd heard from a friend of both of ours that a woman at church was spreading a rumour. Then she looked straight at me.

"She's saying that you and Paul are having an affair, and that God told her so."

The air stopped flowing into my lungs, my heart hammered, and my limbs went limp. I flashed back through the scenes of my life, pulling up the times when I'd legitimately been called out for my sins, and my current law-level innocence became confused with the guilt of my past. The whole time I'd been at the church I'd worried someone would pick up there was something wrong with how I related to Paul, that I was too close–and now I'd left, and the problem was all but resolved, and I hardly saw him anymore—now someone questioned it. And the accusation came from some unstable woman who'd joined the church just before I left and knew nothing. She didn't really know Paul and didn't know me at all. My worry had always been that someone who knew us well would call me on it, would wonder, but not this woman who had attention seeking issues of her own.

Of course, I knew God hadn't told her anything and I couldn't believe anyone had felt it necessary to bring the accusation to me. I wondered what my friend thought I was supposed to do with it. She was looking at me searchingly, and the reason she'd wanted to tell me about it blared out of her face. It seemed she thought the story had merit. I felt sick, betrayed even by her, the carrier of the message.

She continued to watch for any sign it was true, and I felt the guilt wash over me. Oh, I was guilty, just not in the way she thought, and not in any way I could explain to her over lunch, nor would I want to. I fobbed her off, told her what she needed to know but would most likely disbelieve, and as soon as I could I escaped to the privacy of my car.

Panic set in as my thoughts raced, wondering how I might gain control of the situation, yet I knew ultimately what I really wanted to gain control of—the hearts and minds of the people who would most likely hear the rumour—was uncontrollable. I could envision the scrutiny we'd now be under, and I guessed, sadly, the relationship would never be the same.

Six weeks later, I attended the wedding of a young couple from the church. I was aware Paul would be there, along with many people who could quite conceivably have heard the rumour. I tried to block that out, but on the day, as I wandered amongst old acquaintances and friends from church, either I was attracting wariness, or some of them were reacting to what they'd heard.

Of course, I couldn't know which it was, and it was natural or at least easier to believe the rumour was influencing their responses to me. So, I forgot my recent successes and the reality of my lack of guilt, and I let myself develop an attitude. Reject them before they got the chance to reject me. Brazenly, throw their judgment back in their faces. And amid my private little tantrum, a friend asked me to get something he'd left in my car, which I was happy to do. Anything to get away from the condemnation I was feeling.

As I walked out of the driveway heading for my car, Paul was standing next to his vehicle talking with an old friend. They both saw me, and I knew the friend, so I altered course to say hello. Paul watched me appreciatively as I approached, as always, looking like it was a joy to see me, but it was his friend's face that held my attention. All I could see was the accusation. He hadn't smiled when I'd altered course, and in fact, had changed his stance, giving the impression he was going to walk away before I arrived. I don't really know if he was accusing me or I was being overly sensitive, but I began burning, the heat shooting through my limbs, firing me up, ready to physically react to what I saw as provocation.

I wanted to hit back at people in their easy belief in the worst, and I knew just how to do it. Fly full in its face. If they wanted to believe the rumour, I was about to give them all the ammunition they needed. I was in full self-destruct mode. I did what had in the past always come easily, but which I'd had no use for of late. As I walked up the rise towards Paul and his friend, I laid on a bit of swagger in my hips, put a smile on my lips and loaded my eyes with a subtle, "you know you like what you see." I was lashing out, feeling cornered, and I knew I'd hit home, not because of anything Paul did, but because of his friend's reaction. As I arrived at the car, he dropped his eyes and was notably silent, literally shrinking before me, acting like he didn't even know who I was. Paul didn't seem to notice his friend's response, but I was triumphant, resisting the urge to raise my arms and follow him as he walked away, howling my victory over him. And the victory was even more complete because before his friend was out of earshot, Paul had offered to drive me to my car. In your face! That was my attitude as I hopped in the car, still watching the friend walking head down, back into the venue.

Then, a block away, Paul accidentally overran my parked car.

"Of all the cars in the world, I should know yours," he said.

His easy acknowledgment of our close friendship felt good, and I laughed on the inside at the people at the wedding. I knew Paul had heard the rumour, but their judgment hadn't altered his attitude to me one iota. He was still treating me the same way he always had.

Sadly, I wasn't yet acknowledging what had become obvious. Up till then I'd been passing tests with flying colours, but, with me having reverted to old, problematic behaviours, this test had been a definite fail.

Pride Goes Before

In the second semester of that first year of study, the rumour of the affair got to me. My energy levels plummeted, causing my workload to back up, so I turned to one of my lecturers for help. He was a male counsellor, the type of helper that in the past Beth had made clear was strictly forbidden territory, given my tendencies. His response had been immediate, and we quickly met to address my workload. As I trotted out my story, he drew a sharp breath, clearly empathising with the impact the rumour was having. He was caring and understanding. He was nice. It'd been five or six years since I'd noticed Paul was 'too' nice, so in that I could receive the lecturer's kindness without having a problematic response, it felt like a success and an immediate counter to the backward step I'd taken at the wedding.

That first year at college also displayed something I'd been experiencing for a few years and had sometimes ruminated on, but had not found a solid explanation for. Occasionally, I would express an opinion, in this case during lectures, or give an answer, yet I wouldn't know where it'd come from. Couldn't connect one thought to another, couldn't show my working. It suggested the thought didn't come only from me, or indeed, from me at all. It wasn't just that I recognised the wisdom in my own words; it was the incredulous response from others that identified it. People would look at me with wonder in their eyes, clearly taken aback.

And it wasn't only me this happened to. I remember others, particularly one classmate who was the youngest amongst us, saying something that caused us all to exclaim in surprise at the wisdom of her words. I could see that she couldn't believe what she'd said, either. This other worldly wisdom popped up unexpectedly and expressed itself in different ways.

As we moved into that second year of training, things began approaching me from a different angle. I think because of my success with the tests I'd been through. It was as if I had an adversary who, in realising I'd taken ground, had circled around behind me to find a weak point.

We had a new lecturer, a vivacious yet broodingly serious man. During his first lecture, after modeling the work for us, he then had us practice on him. I asked him a series of questions, which he answered, and then he cupped his hand on his chin, elbow resting on the arm folded across his chest, and looked up.

"Are you a counsellor?"

The question surprised me. I thought we were all students, but apparently some were already practicing counsellors and going from a diploma qualification to the degree. I told him I wasn't.

"So, where does your relationship training come from?"

The question both rocked and stroked me. His obvious insinuation that I somehow understood more about what he was teaching than he'd have expected confused me. I didn't know why that would be. I could only imagine it had something to do with my experience in the business, but as time has passed, I understand it was actually this other worldly wisdom. My having received it, though, wasn't about to go unchallenged. As I was leaving his class that day, the lecturer asked a question which set off my old radar. He was standing at the door and as we filed past, our eyes met.

"You get this, don't you?" he said.

I didn't know if I did or not, but I knew the fact he thought so would probably be troublesome for me, and I was right. His question played into all my old patterns. In fact, it highlighted a scene from my life I'd recognised as being a major contributor to my struggle. It'd occurred when I was about nine years old, when my mother had given me a crash course on how to hold a teacher's attention.

She was working at the school where I was a pupil, and after meeting a visiting teacher about to give a lesson to my class, she'd searched me out, telling me to listen attentively when he taught. I understood why, knew it was so he would view me as intelligent, which would reflect well on her. However, she didn't know the long-range impact this little lesson would have on my life. I followed her instructions to the letter, which captured the teacher. He ended up giving much of his lesson directly to me and I felt affirmed, the sense of being able to hold an adult male's attention a powerful drug. I recognised this moment as the seed of the thought pattern that was now turning my current lecturer's attention into a trap for me.

During the six-week gap between my brooding lecturer's block courses, I had a dream. I was attending an event, maybe a wedding, so I was all dressed up. Joey was there, the married man I'd had the affair with in my teens, but he was old now, decrepit, and consigned to a wheelchair. I obviously hadn't expected him to be there and was incredibly pleased to see him. I sat on his knee and snuggled up, resting my cheek in his hands.

I hadn't understood the dream, so I continued down the path I was on. When the lecturer opened the second block of his course, I'd worked myself up to believe I needed to treat him just the way

I had my relationship with Paul. This lecturer needed to think there was "something about Simone" too. I'd even been conscious of the danger, but because I'd come so far, I'd thought it had no teeth, had believed I could get into old patterns and still be okay. I could feel myself running down that familiar track, and when the block course ended, as the class said their goodbyes, I went up and hugged the lecturer. It felt okay to do so. I wasn't the only one, but I saw it brought him up with a round turn. I didn't recognise the look that flashed across his face, but I saw it as a warning. Something about me hugging him hadn't been okay.

"See you soon," he said, which to my mind meant he still thought I was special and that was the important thing. I was happy to think I'd made my mark. It hadn't meant a great deal to me, but it was dangerous thinking, and I should have known better.

Then, just before we began our third and last year of training, I popped into college and, on my way through the foyer, spotted the lecturer coming out of the restroom. I called out to him, feeling sure he'd be pleased to see me, but his response was unexpected. He didn't smile and, in fact, looked as if he wasn't sure who I was. As I got closer, it forced me to adjust my expectation. I'd intended on hugging him, but now I knew that wouldn't happen. I stopped short, embarrassed. My greeting had been friendly, and he was giving nothing in return, and it got worse. He greeted me, though unenthusiastically, and to cover my discomfort, I said the first thing that came into my head.

"This is the big year," I said, meaning it was the last year of the counselling degree, the business end of things. Yet, his retort was short and sharp.

"No, last year was the big year."

It didn't occur to me till later that all his lectures had been in the second year, and he wasn't about to agree with the suggestion they weren't the most important ones. Possibly he was being funny, he was like that, appearing serious but really messing with you, but I wasn't sure. And on the back of his tepid response when he'd seen me, I felt like someone had slapped me.

The good thing was, feeling slapped didn't matter. Sure, I felt it, but I accepted it. Perhaps he'd sensed something of my past weakness and felt threatened. Maybe that was the reason for his less than enthusiastic greeting. Yet I was okay with how I'd responded to his attention. Initially there'd been the reflexive response, wanting him to continue to see me as special, but I had done nothing to insist on it like I would have in the past. I'd not tried to manipulate him. And though it'd been embarrassing when he'd been stand-offish, that had been the end of the matter. I'd spent very little time and energy thinking about it.

I don't believe the unexpected direction this test had come from had been a real threat, but it revealed there was an aspect of the repair process I hadn't fully worked through. It was clear I'd made progress, but I needed to remember Beth's advice from a few years earlier. "It's not about you, what you do he appreciates," she'd told me. I needed to acknowledge where the other worldly wisdom was coming from and not get puffed up by it.

The dream I'd had during that period, the one about Joey, turned out to be a warning. Joey, being old and decrepit, represented the state of my problem. It was old, almost gone, weak and failing, yet my response in the dream had been to fawn over it. I'd been delighted to see Joey, had wanted my lecturer to think there was "something about Simone". I'd sat on my problem's knee, rested my cheek in its hand, so excited to see it I'd snuggled right up to it. Clearly, I hadn't quite put the problem to death.

The last test at college, that I was aware of anyway, had several moving parts. Close to graduation, an issue had arisen with a girl I'd been counselling on one of my placements. Such was the seriousness of the matter I'd had to talk about it with my on-site supervisor, my personal supervisor, and the lecturer who managed our placements. There'd been several discussions, and my personal supervisor was putting pressure on me to make a disclosure to the Police. I was terrified of betraying the trust of my client unnecessarily, and I also believed a disclosure could put her safety at risk.

With my personal supervisor pushing hard, and my on-site supervisor vacillating, I felt pressured. So much so that one day at counselling college, knowing I wouldn't be back for at least a week, I attempted to relieve the pressure by speaking to the lecturer in charge of placements. Unfortunately, she was away and as I didn't want to go another day without talking it through with someone who could help me deal with it; I insisted on seeing one of the other lecturers.

You can imagine my surprise when this other lecturer asked me to meet him at the college café, publicly, with all the other students sitting at tables around us. I wondered if he understood what I wanted to talk about. I decided he couldn't possibly because he was obviously aware I couldn't discuss a client's personal situation with all those people around, so I asked him if he'd mind continuing our conversation in his office. I had some sense he might have been uncomfortable being alone with me, but it quite undid me to discover he was seriously uptight about it. As I followed him to his office, I could feel his hearty displeasure at my having forced his hand, and when we sat down, I got the distinct impression he felt unsafe with me, yet I'd never been a threat to him. Had done nothing even suggestive of such a thing.

I tried to find some evidence to support his behaviour and landed on my memory of a particular paper we'd had to write in our first year of training. In it, I'd been explicit about my past. Could that be why he was so wary? He hadn't been the lecturer in that class though, so there would have to have been some sharing of information. It was the only thing that made sense, that the assignment I'd bared my soul in was producing this wariness, if indeed it was anything outside this man's own personal radar. I didn't really know what to think, but he was about to give me something new to ruminate on, about to confirm his attitude that till that point I'd only guessed at.

"Why did you want to see me?" he said. He didn't mean for me to explain the purpose of the meeting. He meant why had I asked to meet with him in particular? I hadn't and, wow! It amazed me he would position me so blatantly as the dangerous woman. However, I held my own and carefully explained that as the other lecturer was away, I was desperate to talk it through with someone and there'd been nobody else. The situation felt so obvious, but he seemed completely immersed in what he believed of me, so even my answering his question incredulously didn't knock him off the way he was positioning me.

I didn't see it then, but his behaviour was helpful. When he asked why I had to see him, when I'd felt him judge me as the woman trying to take advantage of the man in power, genuine indignation had arisen. Even me telling him the other lecturer was away, that there was nobody else to help, was more of a defensive position than I'd ever mounted before.

So, when I left his office that day, no further ahead with the problem I'd entered it with, and now the implied accusation he'd made adding to the weight I was carrying, that bit of indignation no matter how minor, showed I'd felt unjustly treated. It was reminiscent of what Beth had tried to get me to see years earlier when she'd recommended I watch the movie "Raising Helen" (Marshall, 2004). In it, the protagonist, Helen, fears confrontation, fears the emotional fallout that goes with it, so doesn't react appropriately in meaningful situations, doesn't mount an appropriate defense. Eventually, her love for the children that are unexpectedly placed in her care forces her to push past her fears and aggressively confront what's threatening their continued placement with her. So, someone had judged me, and my reaction had reinforced the most important thing I'd ever heard. My indignation revealed I was dying to myself. I was no longer blowing in the wind, but taking up my position as a new creation in Christ (2 Corinthians 5:17). I was no longer subject to other people's judgment of my past sins, because now I was behaving like a woman who recognised the work Jesus had done to remove them far from me (Psalm 103:12).

The Call Home

During my final year at college, a visiting speaker confessed he'd never fully reconciled his counselling work with his Christianity. His statement got my attention, because in the early years of my relationship with God, one of my favourite authors had been the psychiatrist, Larry Crabb. He'd spent thirty-plus years in the industry and, after all that, had then questioned the impact he'd had with his clients, compared with what a relationship with Jesus would have done for them.

Throughout my counselling training, we students were told not to talk about spiritual things with our clients unless they raised the subject, and it seemed the further we went into our training, the more we wrestled with having to abide by that restriction. When other students had asked me how I felt about it, I'd always glibly replied I had no problem, that I didn't see it as an issue at all. In fact, I considered they were just being good little Christians in thinking there was a problem, that if they couldn't separate the two things, there was something wrong with them. The joke was on me though because, as certain as I'd been that I'd have no trouble with the restriction, I never considered that, like Larry Crabb, I'd do a complete 180 and ask, faced with what Jesus did, what is the worth of counselling, period.

So, it was a surprise when, as soon as I graduated, the discomfort with the profession began. And it didn't just affect my thoughts on counselling, but church, relationships, the whole of my life, really. I'd been so sure I needed to become a counsellor; I'd never fully considered what should follow. I'd assumed the desire to train meant I also had a desire to practice. I'd had an obvious gifting as three friends in the industry and two course instructors had mentioned it to me, and God had pointed me in the direction with the prophecy from Tony Saxon, but I think I got hung up believing because I had a gift and a desire to help people, the logical conclusion was to become a counsellor. Now I questioned whether getting paid to help people in hourly slots, outside the rest of their lived experience, was truly my purpose.

The wrestle started with a general feeling of sadness. I didn't attach it to anything, couldn't say what it was in relation to, but I let myself feel it. I wrote in my journal that maybe it was who I was, and not an emotional response to something I was experiencing. Steve noticed it and responded by becoming more caring and loving, which was interesting, that me being more real with that emotion was drawing out of him the very care and attention I prized in other men. It was as if hiding my feelings of sadness had prevented me from getting the attention I craved from him.

However, despite the sadness, I had to move forward. I was almost phobic about it. It was the beginning of the year; Steve had a new job, and I was pushing myself hard to find counselling work. So, given it was all new beginnings, naturally we started talking about the future, thinking about what our next five years might hold.

"There's no longer a lifestyle reason to stay here," Steve said. "I want to go home." The statement caught me off-guard, perhaps because I hadn't noticed that living in Auckland had, over time, become all about me and Elijah. I'd never considered Steve might want to go back. If anyone had pined for home, it had always been me.

My first thought was the people I'd miss if we went back, but I quickly realized those people were no longer a part of my daily or even weekly existence, so I'd still be able to do that by making a couple of trips to Auckland every year. And as most of our family had either already returned home, my brother from Wellington, Steve's sister from Wales, or they'd never left, I realised we'd be gaining so much more than we'd lose. And as if God agreed and wanted to confirm our thinking, when I settled down to do my bible reading that day, I read in Leviticus about the year of jubilee, when everyone returns home to their family's land.

The sadness coupled with the discussion about going home set me to wondering about my place in the body of Christ too, as in all our talking about leaving Auckland, leaving the church I'd been attending in the latter years of my degree hadn't once come up.

That Sunday the pastor got people to testify about the scriptures that had impacted them over the Christmas holidays, so of course, I'd been in Leviticus, and in Numbers too actually. I'd learned everyone was numbered, and each tribe had its place around the tabernacle. God had been very specific about where he placed each tribe and their numbers, and I realized He was showing me He also had a specific place for me within His body of believers.

Then in the early hours of the morning on the 12th of February, it came to me, seemingly an answer to all my ruminations about church, counselling, and calling. The answer I received seemed to encompass all strands of my thinking in one. It centered on purpose. I realised I needed to write down my testimony, and that's exactly how I expressed the thought in my journal. It was as if, up till that moment, I'd forgotten the prophetic word I'd received four years earlier, the one that had blatantly told me, "Tell your story, write it down so people can run with it."

Come Out

2014

The sadness in relation to my counselling journey was only the beginning of the upheaval. I'd studied and practiced my trade for three years, with never a shred of doubt I was doing the right thing, and now I didn't have any idea which direction to head. Of course, I couldn't know there was a whole process I'd have to go through to find my way forward. And such was the mess in my head that even with a big question mark over counselling as a career, I was adamant I had to get a job, and I knew it was going to take some massaging to achieve that.

Counselling positions came up, but mostly in schools, so poorly paid unless you had a teaching degree, and at a rate of five hundred students to one counsellor, that work could be very stressful. I'd done three placements in schools, so I was familiar with it. I knew it wasn't something I wanted to pursue. Fortunately, I'd connected with the manager of a local agency and though it happened in a round-a-bout way, with one of their counsellors having an accident, they offered me a part time position to help tide them over till she got back on her feet.

However, rather than finding relief in getting a job, something I'd believed to be quite difficult to achieve, within the first few weeks, I was struggling. I was unusually tired, wasn't sleeping and not journaling regularly, a sure sign I wasn't processing. And though I desperately needed a chiropractic adjustment, I didn't make an appointment because I had no energy to fight the traffic to get there. Of course, my counselling work suffered. I was forgetting things, and then when I'd realise, usually soon after, so there was still time to rectify the situation, I'd be apoplectic with myself. It was a response completely out of proportion with what I'd forgotten to do.

And there were so many things I couldn't reconcile. I loved sitting with clients, hearing their stories and helping them gain a greater sense of agency, but I was avoiding myself by concentrating on their stuff. I'd made a revealing note about it in my journal, that "seemingly, counselling shuts me up." I also loved being a part of such a large team of social workers. It was a joy to be surrounded by such compassionate people, yet I disliked spending time away from home. I'd wake in the mornings already stressed about nothing, my body on edge, then I'd hate leaving for work, a problem not helped when someone stole my car, leaving me scrambling for transport for two months. And then when I was at work, because the agency was outgrowing its site, there was, in part, a sense I was unwelcome. I was the temporary employee, and the cramped working conditions meant they were regularly shifting me around within the office to make room for the permanent staff.

At church, the pastor spoke about dreams, that recurring ones meant something in your life was unresolved. If that were true, I had something going on because four times I dreamt some version of losing my purse, or having what was in it stolen. And yes, I connected it to the song "Money, Money, Money" which had accompanied Greg Burson's prophetic word for me. I knew I needed to work out what God was highlighting.

If I thought about what money represented, it was a way of obtaining paradise apart from God. Therefore, I wondered if the dreams were telling me I'd put my trust in a fallible god. There was the warning in scripture about the rich fool storing up his wealth so he can live at ease, with no consideration of God. Then when he dies, and his soul is required of him, God tells him he's a fool, and asks who gets all he's provided now (Luke 12:16-21)? It seemed God was showing me my insistence that I get a counselling job straight out of college, and my stress with the work, they were attempts to look after myself, to keep myself safe. It was my way of protecting and providing, doing things in my own strength, my way. All evidence I didn't trust Him.

My past attempts to know Paul had been the same thing. I'd immersed myself in his world so I could be there to meet his needs, a perverted version of God's plan. It hadn't been Paul's world I needed to know, but God's will, His kingdom. My needs had led me to put people like Paul or Beth in God's place. Those people had been in my life to help me grow, but God had known I'd lean on them too much. He'd placed them there to do a work, and once they'd done it, He took them away. Now I needed to work solely with Him, to find more fullness in His and my relationship. I could see, in my head anyway, maybe not yet my heart, that my relationship with Him needed to be foremost in my life.

I picked up Gerald May's book, *The Dark Night of the Soul* (2004). He talked about relinquishing our attachments, the things we cling to instead of God, about the numbness they create between Him and us, as if we're dealing with Him through a veil. I had some sense that this knowledge was moving from my head to my heart, that I was reaching the end of myself, the end of my attempts to control everything. But I still had things I needed to put away.

There was a tape that played in my head telling me, you need to do more, you should be achieving, making it happen. I heard it when the pastor praised someone in the congregation, I heard it when someone asked what I did with my time outside of work, I heard it when Paul told me he thought people used the concept of 'the dark night of the soul' as an excuse. I even heard it in my insistence I get a job straight out of counselling college. What's more interesting is where I didn't hear it; in my relationship with the Lord or in the needs of my son. In fact, in relation to my son, I heard I need to do less so I have more time for him, and in relation to the Lord, I heard I needed to be still (The New International Version Study Bible 1973/1985, Psalm 46:10).

It sounds ridiculous because if you took it at face value, it appeared I put my trust in others. I'd once said to Beth that I 'kinged' people in my life. Her response had been to suggest that a more apt description was that I 'queened' myself. Because what looked like trust was a bait and switch. I appeared to be following a person's lead, when the relationship actually centred on my ability to manipulate them, to be the one in control. And when I didn't feel that I was in control, I would shake, tremble, like I had during my first experiences of the presence of God. It was all a refusal to trust in something other than myself. I couldn't risk that sort of reliance, so I didn't initiate with God, but waited for Him to come to me. I'm the "one who listens", that's what my name means. I wasn't straight with Him about what I wanted, I didn't ask. When I felt life wasn't going well, I'd fix my weight, or develop a five or a ten-year plan. I'd always insisted on my independent solutions, had wanted things my way, to be the one in control. But now I was in a new time, new things were coming to pass.

"Press on, come on, walk with Me," I heard Him say.

I cried out in my heart, Lord, how? I heard through scripture that He had declared new things, but before I'd see them, He'd proclaim them to me (Isaiah 42:9). I realised He'd already proclaimed the new things. I'd already received His word, had been told by the prophets Saxon and Burson to "speak to the Prodigals, the ones whose hearts are far from the Lord", and "to tell my story, it's a great demonstration of the Gospel." And God had more to say, telling me that what I heard whispered in my ear was to be widely proclaimed (Matthew 10:27). He wanted me to rely on Jesus, to lean on Him, not the plenty or the lack in my personal resources. But I felt hindered, and He had a response for that too. He told me that though "My flesh and my heart may fail," He was "the strength of my heart and my portion forever" (Psalm 73:26).

It was a call for me to walk in faith. Yet I wanted to defend myself against the perceptions of others, perhaps like the Pharisees who kept the outside of the cup clean, yet the inside was full of robbery and self-interest (Matthew 23:25). They did things that made them look like they had it all together, and Jesus was most severe with them. I believe it was because they misrepresented Him, presented as a clean cup, yet inside they were filthy. What I was called to do threatened how others would perceive me, and I had to get past that.

When I looked at my life, I saw the insatiableness of my chase after comfort. The hurt was there for that reason, to turn me to Him. In scripture, God uses metaphor to describe this chase after the counterfeit, often referring to it as adultery. In the chasing I'd felt a satiety, but what needed sating, although quieted somewhat, would eventually come back stronger than ever. The words of the prophet Tony Saxon spoke to me about it:

> You will define things differently in yourself, in your past, ... your current situations ... because God has and will continue to refashion your mind so that your words have power to them, so that when you speak to people, you will be able to say to them, in comfort and in truth, "this is not worthless, this is precious."

Then it came to me, the understanding that life in Him has set me free. I was being taught to see things differently. The hunger I'd felt to be needed and affirmed by Paul, and others, it was a counterfeit. Not the hunger itself, but those people I set my sights on. I'd been going after a fake. I'd taken the desire for God that was in me, the very highest desire, and the one God wanted to find in my heart, and I'd perverted it. But God was showing me the desire itself, the hunger I had for a King, the true King, that wasn't worthless. That was precious.

He'd told me I was to "speak to the prodigals" and I'd always wondered who they were, had used not knowing as an excuse. How could I speak to them if I didn't know who they were? I'd noted, based on the story of the Prodigal Son, that they were people who took their inheritance early, who lived a life of excess and pleasure, then ended up living with pigs and eating their leftovers. They were the ones who, like me, had gone racing off after other gods. It suggested a demand for "paradise" outside of God and His timing.

I'd often noticed how prophets in the bible had to go through some form of the word they were called to bring. Perhaps the prime example was the prophet Hosea, who was called to speak of God's love for the wayward Israelites, which was perfectly paralleled in his marriage to the unfaithful Gomer. Not that I considered myself a prophet, but it seemed I'd been called to bring something of the knowledge of God to people. Of course, I identified with living a life of excess and pleasure. I'd demanded my own way and had ended up in a downward spiral. I'd felt the destructive nature of my actions and driven myself into a corner by seeking pleasure and comfort in all the wrong places. I noted in *The Dark Night of the Soul* (May, 2004) that what follows the dark night is the morning light. It frees you from your attachments so you can pursue what your heart truly desires.

I thought about the time I'd learned that being freed from attachments was a possibility. God had known I needed more help to believe. I'd been in our bedroom with the door closed, pressing in with Him, desperate to want His way but still feeling I wasn't winning the fight. I was wrestling, and then as if something had entered the room there'd been a change in the atmosphere, and I'd had a sense of being lifted above the bed. I was no longer in my room and there was a presence, an impression of being surrounded by gold, and the feeling of complete freedom, like nothing had any power over me.

With attachments, addictions, or obsessions, there's always a sense of being pulled or driven, constantly harried in the way a dog worries a sheep (interesting analogy). My attachments had tossed me back and forth, but in this vision, I sensed nothing in or of the world had any power over me. It was brief, and I was swiftly back in this realm with all its attachments, but it left me with an experience of a freedom I imagine will eventually be permanent. It gave me a glimpse of what we put up with, what we allow to hold us back. Yet

I understood that as a follower of Jesus, I didn't need to put up with it, that there was a better way.

Interestingly, it was during all this that Paul left Auckland, shifted away. It felt like the end of an era. He came to say goodbye, but it was a hurried time as he had a friend waiting for him, and I felt no satisfaction in it. I had the sense I was losing something of myself, disappearing, but as I sat with the feeling, I realized it spoke to my fear of man, the people pleasing, the idolising that God wanted me to put to death.

Paul briefly returned some months later for a wedding, and what struck me was how disconnected I felt to him, and to the community I'd previously considered my own. For me it had all centred on my need to be needed, my desire to be indispensable to him, and in that I no longer wanted or needed that, I felt the whole group of people were not a part of the life I had going forward. I stood in the parking lot at the end of the event, having just said goodbye to Paul, and as I watched him drive off, I had a feeling of complete peace. I remembered how I'd spent so much time scanning passing traffic looking for him in his old car, had memorised his number plate, always hoping to spot it so I could know where the object of my obsession was. And now, I was watching him drive away in a different car, and it was jarring. I felt sad at the change of his importance in my life, someone I'd held great affection for, still did, but it felt so right to be letting go of the demandingness that it had held. I sighed heavily, released the weight of it, got in my car, and headed home.

And on the heels of this came the understanding that the dream I'd had about the horse going crazy in the paddock, getting caught in the fence, the wire forming a noose around my neck and me yelling at my father to bring the wire cutters and him tarrying in response ... I'd been right. It wasn't about my father, not in the way I'd always believed. No, it was about my need to satisfy my heart's desire for God the Father by using man, seeking someone to put in God's place. It was about idolatry, or the way God often referred to it, adultery. Humankind was not my provider, my protector, my saviour. They could never be all that I needed.

The culmination of it all was now it was time to come out. Of Auckland, of church, of counselling, and of unhealthy ways of relating. Out of all the things that kept me from God and His will for my life.

Rise Up

2015

We'd got a new Rottweiler, Riley, a confident pup who loved Indy, our older dog. I got up early each morning to take them out to the toilet and then I'd write three pages in my journal. It was a way of priming the pump, stirring up my writing ability, and it showed me what I liked to write about. I noticed I didn't talk about events as much as I did the emotions that surrounded them, mine and those of the people in my life. I seemed to place the greatest weight on the feelings I experienced and maybe I shouldn't have, but I had a high trust in my ability to sense what was going on through what I felt, rather than what I thought, or reason told me.

As I practiced, the things I wrote about brought further confirmation I was to tell my story, and that it would focus on my inner world. But the nature of what I'd battled through meant I felt some reluctance to expose myself. My story was hardly the most flattering tale. I also struggled with how I was to present it, and in my search for the best way, I read *Your Life as Story: Discovering the "New Autobiography" and Writing Memoir as Literature* (Rainer, 1997). The author Rainer shared excerpts from many memoirs, and in that most of the stories displayed some of the more challenging issues in life, I realised I too had to present my knowing. If I didn't, I'd be performing a disservice in the world. So even though the self-doubt ran rampant, I came to understand that if I judged my 'I' as unpalatable, I was judging God. He had been explicit. "Tell your story so that others can run with it." So, it wasn't about me and my comfort levels. I wasn't to decide the value of what I had to say, or whether the world was ready to hear it. I didn't even have to think it was a good story. I just had to be obedient to the call, to the desire to write what rose up in me. Beyond that was none of my business.

I compared my need to share my story of adultery with the world's feelings on the subject. Even Dr. Phil of afternoon talk show fame seemed to have a bit of an attitude towards adulterers, yet he considered himself to be the most accepting person you were ever likely to meet. Of course, maybe in his position keeping a little distance was appropriate. But I could see God's attitude was wholly different, as evidenced in His cry to the unfaithful Israelites in the book of Hosea. He laments, asking them how He could give them up to the fate of Sodom and Gomorrah, cities destroyed with brimstone and fire because of their depravity. God tells the Israelites His heart is upturned and all His compassion is called forth (Hosea 11:8). He refuses to execute His anger against them, explaining that He can't because He's not man, He's God, and He believes His sons will come back to Him trembling when He roars (Hosea 11:9-10). In Hosea's time, the Israelites were being ruled by Assyria because they refused to return to God. I'd been told I was to speak to the prodigals, the ones whose hearts were far from God. I'd also been told I would roar. I wondered, was I to roar for God in His compassion for His people?

It seemed tangential. Maybe it was, maybe it wasn't, but death had also been on my mind for a while. Not because there was any obvious threat, but more because I was waiting for the next one to drop, could feel it coming and felt it would be easier to cope with if I was ready and waiting when it happened. It occurred to me it was loss I feared. It didn't occur to me that what I greatly feared might come upon me (Job 3:25).

The puppy woke me at 5am one morning, so I took him out, then put him back to bed and slept till nearly 8am. The sleep in felt like a win given his whining during the night had been keeping us awake for a week. I wrote my three pages in my journal while he tore strips off the Sultana Bran box that Steve had put down for him to play with. The mess added to the Nutri Grain box he'd ripped up the day before. I didn't really know what I was doing in terms of the writing. I was just feeling my way through. What I knew was writing and family were my whole life now. I'd stopped going to church, and I wasn't counselling. I'd removed everything that didn't seem to be what I was called to do.

My friend Abby had said a few months earlier that what I would do next would be all about me and God, not joining what someone else was doing. She'd prophesied:

Rise up, oh woman of God, clothed in strength, beauty, glory … rise up into the things that God has for you. He's already clothed you in strength, come right out of where you have been. Walk in faith, at a new level, above the earth, in faith, taking from Him what you need—you can only walk that way with Him. He's blessed you with gifts you've not been using. He's got other gifts for you to lay hold of, to take and do. Leave it behind, whatever it is. He's already clothed you, made you strong, you are beautiful. Don't be hindered, be where you can be free to operate at your highest level. Break free.

I wasn't sure writing was what the word referred to, but I was open to it. I couldn't deny the way it fit with all that God had said to me, and the way it meshed with how I liked to live. It was a battle, though, descending into deep places, exploring feelings that were emotionally heavy. But I felt it was my inner world I was to bring to life, the way I'd related to myself and to God, how that had played out.

It was necessary to discipline myself to write each day as a way of developing my ability, even if it was only in my journal. It wasn't a hardship as I enjoyed being at home, the solitude, exploring emotions, naming and ordering my experience. And looking ahead, the thought of completing my book, holding it in my hands, and having it impact others, it was exciting. I could feel the sense of accomplishment I'd get when I achieved what I'd been called to do. And the depth of desire I had in leaving something of myself on the page, to be known, to catch what has and is going on in my being, that held great joy. I knew I needed to collect what flowed through me, and I wondered if that had been the experience of those who'd penned the Scriptures.

Through What We Suffer

In my last year at counselling college, I'd argued with one of my lecturers for an hour and a half. Earlier, at the beginning of the semester, she'd been vulnerable with the class; had told us a very difficult thing she'd had to endure in her life, and based on her transparency I'd thought the stage was set for great wrestling and learning, that I'd really love her class. But the opposite had been true. She'd developed a theology around her suffering that I found offensive. Not to me, but to God, and that's what led to the argument.

She'd told us a loving God wouldn't allow what had happened to her, therefore God wasn't in it, was not present for it. I couldn't countenance such a position, that God doesn't know about, or has no interest in the difficult things we experience. That somehow, He wouldn't use them to bring good, for His purposes. I don't think He's the cause of them, but I am certain He's working amongst them.

The lecturer and I could not reach common ground, and in the end, we parted amicably, agreeing to disagree. But as I left her office, I saw the confusion on her face, and I felt it was because I'd held so strongly to what I believed despite her powerful position as the lecturer, or 'expert'. I think it rattled her. I'd noticed her tendency to be all about the young people on campus and I wondered if she'd been deliberately avoiding those more liable to question her belief system. Not that I think my challenge altered her position, just that she might have been more open to a different perspective. I had no clue I was going to have to stand on what I believed so soon after, though, granted, my experience of loss was not anywhere near her level. But I was going to have to live out my theology.

I first noticed the puppy was sick at the beginning of February when, during his training, I had to pull on the leash to get him to keep up with me, like he was especially tired. Then he spent much of the next day lying on the cool tiles in the hallway. It was the hottest month of the year, and he was a puppy, so I explained it away as him not being able to handle the heat. Then I noticed him standing alone up the back of our property, nose poked in the air, ears fluttering in the wind, and somehow, I knew something was different.

Later, when he vomited in the family room, a purple red substance, I should have known it meant his vomit had blood in it, but I just assumed he'd eaten something bad. However, when I took him to the vet, they guessed he had Parvo Virus, but couldn't confirm it because they'd run out of test kits. Unbeknownst to us, there'd been an outbreak in our area.

So, began a horrendous week. The first two nights, I was up every hour to give the puppy saline. The third night we left him overnight at the vets, just so I could get some sleep, and then I continued my vigil. And I was successful. He survived the initial onslaught of that first week, but while I'd been trying to keep him alive, the disease had infiltrated his body in ways no one expected. He was enduring terrible pain in his hip, couldn't move without yelping in a scream like fashion, and the vet had no explanation. And what they wanted to do for him felt more exploratory than an attempt to fix it. They didn't know what was wrong, and that wasn't good enough. I couldn't let him suffer any more. On Valentine's Day at nine in the morning, I took him to the vet for the last time.

I easily remembered the things I'd done which had signed his death warrant. They pounded in my memory. I'd forgotten what we'd been told by the vet when our older dog had been a puppy, that you don't take them off your property until they're six months old. So, I'd been walking Riley in the park. And we hadn't been reading the local paper, which had alerted dog owners to the high risk in our area. And the clincher. Six weeks earlier I'd picked up Riley's puppy record and felt a prod—so much so I can still remember it, but I'd actively decided against responding. I'd been aware I was taking a risk, yet I'd put his vaccination book back in the cupboard, knowing he was due his shots, but telling myself he didn't need them. In fact, the thought process went deeper. We'd chosen not to have our son vaccinated either, believing that vaccinations sometimes have catastrophic negative effects and far-reaching health implications. The situation with Riley didn't disavow me of that thinking. I was just disappointed in my failure to take other protective actions.

Riley had certainly captured my heart, causing all our other animals to take a back seat. Now I wouldn't get to watch him grow up and enjoy life, lying flat out as puppies do, or growling and jumping all over Indy. I'd no longer see the splat of his huge puppy paws hitting the ground with careless abandon, the ruffle of his floppy, Setter-like ears, or his legs poking out like drumsticks as he lay doggie-paddle style under the lounge chairs.

His death brought the loss of a dog I'd really thought I would enjoy. I tried to console myself with the logic of what the reality had been for him, that in the end all he was experiencing was pain, and now it was over. It was that pain which had caused me to pray for him on the eve of Valentine's Day, to ask for a miracle. Then, during those last few minutes at the vet's while we waited in the back of the car for his appointment, he appeared to be momentarily pain free. I was stroking his head, and he was interested in his surroundings, the other dogs coming and going, and growling at a man who came too close to the car. He seemed to be really enjoying the cuddle, and maybe that was the answer to my prayer. The miracle being his last half hour of life pain free, not knowing what was coming, that he'd never wake up again.

He looked beautiful, his head so intelligent, making him seem far older than his four and a half months. Probably the pain had done that to him. Then inside the vet clinic, I placed him on the bench on a soft rug the vet had laid out for him. He was no longer with it as the sedative had kicked in. I was just telling him what a good boy he'd been, that I was sorry, he shouldn't have had to go through it, and he growled. I know he wasn't with it, but it was like an ending, a 'let me go'. And I did. I knocked on the door, the signal to let the vet know it was time. She was so gentle with him; he wouldn't have known anything. I remember how I'd been waiting for the next death to drop, never thinking I would feel so responsible for it.

Losing him caused me to want to go deeper, to challenge myself. Did it all come back to control? Did I feel I'd lost it because I'd been unable to administrate every moment with Riley? Had I really believed I could avoid the pain if I prepared myself for the next death? I think the reality was the curtain of illusion had drawn back to reveal my inability to effectively control the world at all.

I'd spent my life trying to control my environment, manipulating people and situations. I'd done it because I thought

I was the best person to keep myself safe, whether as the one in charge, or being able to pull the strings of that person. But suddenly I understood that no matter my best efforts, no matter which way I jumped, things could end badly. Vaccinating the dog could have caused damage—it happens. I'd always suspected it had with my cat, yet not vaccinating the dog had also been tragic. I was finally seeing the truth in high definition—I had no control over the safety of my world. My human striving would never achieve what I wanted. I could not guarantee the prevention of loss, could not guarantee my safety, nor the satisfaction of all my needs. Try as I might to manage every moment, to exert as much control over the world as I could, I'd never be able to provide myself with paradise.

When the pain of realisation hit it was like I'd lanced an infected wound. In letting go of my belief in my ability to control life, the sorrow had poured out. It wasn't just sorrow for Riley, but years of pain I'd held up behind the dam I'd erected. My refusal to feel the pain, aka my manipulative ways, had been the wall my obsessions had hidden behind.

When I'd been on the farm, sometimes I'd gone riding all day with my friend Lisa. Such relaxed enjoyment had come easily to her, but for me it'd been more difficult. I'd had to wrestle with myself so I could 'let go'. To do it had been an achievement. Lisa had more of a 'come what may' attitude to life, and I've noticed over the years how much I enjoy being around people who don't find it necessary to manage every moment. They seem to have the freedom to seek life wherever and whenever it's available, not restricting their time because of what the clock says, or the expectations of others. They don't need to be in control to feel safe. It seemed this thought pathway was opening me up to the message God had for me, that He and I can't both run the show.

I had once made a flippant statement that, "life is about loss." But I hadn't really understood what I was saying. See, I'd always assumed I had a right to have my needs met, and to make that happen if necessary. That if I lacked, I had every right to go after filling that lack for myself. I hadn't believed I could do something illegal, but obviously not placed that same restriction on the immoral. I'd been all about protecting myself, shoring up, not just casually accepting loss when it came, as my flippant statement implied. But now I could see the pain of loss, the sorrow, it wasn't my cue to go out and get what I felt I needed to quell it as I'd done in the past. No, it was to be felt, it needed to be. It was the work of emotions. They are designed to heal.

I will always have unsatisfied desire and loss, I am not to hide from it, I need to feel the pain. As my mentor Beth said, God is taking me through it, so I'm in the reality of Him more. The fullness is not yet. Feeling the sorrow for Riley confirmed I wasn't in control. It caused me to loosen my grip on life, and far from needing to exclude the pain at all cost, I was to embrace it. And in removing the dam of control and embracing the pain, the healing flowed.

Joining Up

Not long after the death of Riley, I had the sense the last of the battle was over, the one that'd begun so many years earlier when I'd ridden Cloudy to the end of the road, to where the man from the marae lived. I felt I was emerging from the swamp clean and white, that it was over, this thing that had been a part of my life for so long.

I was in a period of simply basking in God as He continued to respond to me, in the moment gentle and kind, calling me to lay everything down and allow Him to lead. I felt His presence within, His life, a knowing rather than something I could grasp and attach anything to. It seemed this was how God deals with us. In all our desire for attachment, He's completely counter, giving us nothing to take hold of and mould into our own version of Him. Seek and we find (Matthew 7:7), yes, but there is always seeking. I don't find Him in the exact place I left Him. In fact, if I knew that by performing disciplines a certain way I could bend God to my will, I'd be in control again, and I know exactly where that leads. However, He's not a tease, offering and never quite fulfilling on the promise. When I sought, I found. He is generous in a way that is beyond my understanding and has given a return on my seeking far beyond what I would've expected.

I remember at my graduation wearing an eye-catching lemon, lime, and grey dress. Years earlier, I'd complained in my heart that in working alongside the youth, somehow, they'd never caught me in any of the copious photos posted on Facebook. I know it sounds whiney, but it'd caused me to question whether I was visible, whether I was being seen. The same thing had happened when the counselling college had taken marketing photos. They chose me as a model, but only my left hand made the cut. Yet on graduation day, the photographer took multiple shots of me, and put one of them on the front page of the website. I knew it was God being God. It says so much about who He is. He heard my heart, even though I never voiced the complaint. In a similar instance of His surprising goodness friends had shown us through a house, and in my heart, I'd said, 'Why can't we have a house like this?' It had only been a matter of weeks, and we were living in that very house, rent free. God loves to surprise and amaze His children.

I think my struggle to believe in the goodness of God has been in part because of my need to control, which has cultivated an independent spirit, and that spirit has told me that the good things in life come through your own effort. In the business there was a saying. "If it is to be, it's up to me." I had always heartily agreed with that, had never felt worthy of a return greater than what I put in. That thinking has meant I've never felt worthy of being treated like a daughter. A father always wants to give good gifts to His children, yet I'd cast myself as an employee, receiving only that which I'd worked for. I can remember the indignation I'd felt when my mother gave her friend's son the same gifts for Christmas that she gave my son. I understood she wanted her friends to have their child valued as a grandchild, but she failed to think of what it said to me and my son. So, I could see the problem in relation to him, but it's taken a while for me to see it for myself. Beth always encouraged me to see God in all the different ways He presents, but primarily as my loving Father. It's taken time and Him showing me again and again His desire to give me good gifts, but eventually I've come to a place of trusting in His goodness.

Of course, discovering I'd come to the end of my battle wasn't instant, but the release covered all aspects of me and went on for months, with the death of Riley playing the role of the last straw. This was the grief of a lifetime being experienced all at once. I battled different sicknesses, each lasting for weeks at a time as my physical self, along with my emotional and spiritual, broke down. Mentally and emotionally, I came to a halt for a few months, unable to do anything but what was necessary. I dragged myself through the days, slept a lot, or just sat and thought, and yes, I recognise it was fortunate I could do so, and I guessed that was God's doing too. He'd led me through, been in it with me, and now He was making sure I had the peace and time needed to rejuvenate.

While I did that, I was still being taught, learning more about God's perspective through my interactions with people. When I told my grandmother I'd had to have Riley put down, rather than letting me talk, she'd launched into a story about the dog she'd had years earlier. And my father, when I told him I'd been unwell, had interjected, "Let me stop you right there," and then had spoken at length about someone he knew who'd been unwell and had juiced their way back to health. Then when I rang him to find out how his holiday had gone, he'd talked about it for twenty minutes, yet when I began telling him about how things were at my end, he couldn't get off the phone fast enough. And my mother, busy telling me about how she and her husband went here and there, did this 'n' that, and because my world was more cerebral, it didn't seem to interest her. We shared little common ground, or so I thought, and maybe it was more I wasn't putting myself out there, fearing her lack of interest if I really showed who I was. And then there was Paul. When he'd ring, the conversation would be all about him. And perhaps it wasn't that there was no room for me, but again, I was reticent to insert myself into the conversation. I felt he couldn't relate to the things that interested me, which I suspected was because we'd always related around the things he was interested in.

Although all of this led me to question whether I was boring, or if I driveled on, what I really thought was they didn't know who I was now, or even want to, and maybe it was a necessary contrast. God was showing me humanity could never fully meet my need, couldn't keep up with all the change I'd been through, and maybe it's contrary to His purpose if they do.

As time went on, I gradually returned to concentrating on writing my three pages, and as the theme of what I was writing revealed itself, this time it was clear I was writing the story of my life and how I saw God moving in it. And I was learning just how well He knew me. I was searching through my journals for the story I was to tell, and the evidence was piling up. God is always and has always been actively working in my life. Everything that has happened and is happening, the choices I've made and will make, He is and has been involved. And everything that goes on and has gone on has served His end game, of bringing all things for good, yet all without violating my free will.

Reflecting on these things, I saw Him as gentle, breathing into situations, not strong-arming them, whispering in my ear, not hitting me over the head with a four-by-two. And He was patient, far more than I was with myself or others. When I thought of Him doing and being this way in my life, I realized I hadn't had it in my relationship with my earthly father. He'd never really known me.

Yet of course there was lack, the point being, no man can fill God's role in our life. It was the very thing God wanted me to understand. It was as the prophet had said, '[my] complaint is my vision'.

It was my parent's lack of knowledge of me, how unknown I'd felt, which was my complaint. Because they'd not known me, they'd not been there for me emotionally, and more than that, no one had stepped up to fill the gap. However, my complaint was not without its finger pointing back at me. I realise my independent, self-serving response to my parent's lack had created the conditions which had made it difficult for people to step in and fill at least some of the role my parents had failed to play. Which had, of course, left every opportunity for the wrong ones to step in.

So, God has shown Himself to be the complete contrast to all others; intimately acquainted with my life. His timing has been perfect, with the right helper crossing my path when I was ready to change, when He'd spoken to me through my dreams they'd been about horses, and the prophecies He'd given always had something in them that no one else knew about me. His calling card, if you will. And even now He'd eased me into the knowledge of the control I'd been exerting on life, yet He hadn't condemned me, but had waited till I was ready to hear. I felt Him wanting to be with me, waiting for me to reach new levels in my knowledge of Him so we could enjoy greater intimacy.

And key in this whole process were my emotions. So often they're maligned, particularly in the church, it seems, because it's true they shouldn't rule. But in the hurry to encourage their oppression, maybe we've lost our insight into the work they do, or maybe we've never fully known their importance. During the years when I discovered I needed to let myself feel the emotions that arose, that they were healing, what I noticed was they performed a work in me, they did a good thing. What I hadn't known was what that good thing was. Now I see our emotions reveal the true desires of our heart. They allow us to fully engage with all that God has provided. It's our refusal to feel them that causes problems.

I had been an addict. I believe it's accepted that addicts become that way to prevent themselves from feeling emotional pain. The emotion they're avoiding varies. It turns out, knowing God requires emotional engagement. Only in delighting in all that God provides, in really feeling and experiencing the fullness of life, did the true desire of my heart show itself. It was only in welcoming His influence, truly trusting He is good and allowing myself to feel the emotions that arose in me, have I grown in intimacy with Him. It's as if the revelation of your heart's desire lives in the degree to which you're willing to abandon yourself to His way, to enjoy the fullness of Him.

I wonder if it's like horse whispering, if that is a simpler version of what goes on between humankind and God. Man enters the yard, the bounded place, and skitters around running up to the fences, panicking. God just stands there, and when man stops, He moves towards him, at which point man runs again, till eventually he can't escape the boundaries God has set and starts moving towards Him, running up to Him and then running away. When man finally realises that being close to God feels safe, he latches on and everywhere God goes, man goes too.

Horse whisperer, Monty Roberts, talks about 'join up', speaks about that being the heart of the young horse. It's what he desperately needs to feel safe and content. The lead mare trains him using isolation from herself and the herd as a curb for bad behaviour. I think I could make a case that this happens amongst humankind too. 'Join up' for humans, I think, is walking with our

God. All our grasping, our arranging for our needs to be met, leads away from that. What He's written on our hearts will turn us towards 'join up' if we surrender to it. It's in our recognising He is offering what we truly desire, that we stop trying to arrange for it.

In true to life fashion, though, things don't stay the same, and my heart goes from being fully open to God back to feeling a little numb. The closeness alters slightly; I think so I learn that to experience it, I need to be present to it. My inattention causes it to wane, yet my attentiveness enlivens it almost immediately. There's anticipation, wanting and longing with it, excitement too. And peace. It's a gentle presence and I love it, but I have a sense of not always knowing how to be with it. I think that is again about letting go.

We had to take Indy, our older dog, to the vet and, of course, I was reticent to engage with the staff there, the sadness of the loss of Riley flooding back in. And then because I had to leave Indy with them, the feelings from the last time I left a dog there returned. Weeks later, after multiple visits to the vet, we got the diagnosis. Indy had lung cancer. I'd known something was wrong, had done for months, but had not wanted to believe it. He looked old and had become that way overnight.

It's strange, the things that motivate us. Indy had to be put down too and losing him just months after Riley forced us to act on the decision we'd made. We'd talked about going home, had decided we were going home at some point, but now we were doing it. Steve actively began looking for work that would allow us to move back, and in the end, it was easy. The thing that had probably held us back the most, Elijah, we knew he'd just have to deal with it. There were greater factors at play than his comfort level. And then God put the icing on top of our decision. When Steve mentioned he was looking for work back home, his boss asked him whether he'd consider working for them remotely, and two weeks later, it was all done and dusted. Job sorted, house on the market, and the search for a new property in our hometown begun.

Remembering

2016

We grabbed our hats and coats, loaded Kobe, our one-year-old Rottweiler, into the back of the car, and headed for the beach. It was cold, the middle of the year in the southern hemisphere. The light seemed shadowed, bright in our eyes because the sun was lower in the sky, but tempered, as if the earth were wearing a hat and we were peering out beneath its brim.

When we arrived, as we unloaded the dog, the wind pushed and pulled at us, wrestling with the trees that lined the car park, creating a barrage of rattling, leaf on leaf action. I wrapped myself in a thick coat and pulled on a woolly hat. Steve only needed his jacket to fend off the chill. We walked down the stony track to the beach, leaving Kobe off leash, free to enjoy himself. He bounded up to us and then raced away, busying himself snuffling at the ground and lifting his leg here and there, his erratic movements suggesting he believed his investigating options were far greater than the time he had available.

As the metal track gave way to sand, we could hear the waves crashing on the shore, and eventually the track opened to dunes. As we came over a slight rise, the ocean stretched out before us, and the wind started its battering, whipping our breath and words straight from our mouths. But the sun was still strong, providing welcome warmth and making the wind's chilling efforts bearable.

Behind us was the surf lifesaving club, and to our right the beach stretching a few hundred metres to rocks that led up a steep hill. To our left there was another several hundred metres of beach, ending in rocks and a steep dune that Elijah had spent several summer days rolling down when he was younger. The sand sloped away in front of us, meeting the foamy waves racing up the shore. Kobe had never seen the ocean and as we walked down the sand dunes onto the beach he darted towards the waves as they receded, biting at the foam, and then just as quickly tucking the nub of his tail in behind him and scampering back as a fresh set rolled in. I ran into the wake of the water, encouraging him, but the waves sent me back just as quickly. Kobe barked and feinted left and right, his ears pulled back, his bark swallowed by the wind. I spread my arms out and tilted my face to the sun, somehow feeling young again. I could almost taste what it felt like for the wind to stir me into running, just for the joy of it. In fact, I ran the slightly manufactured run of those who no longer do a lot. It was short-lived—disappointing, even. It didn't take long to wear out, especially with the added weight of my winter woollies. Eventually, Steve put his arm around me, and we wandered along the waterline.

It was the middle of the week and the middle of winter, so we had the beach to ourselves. As we walked, we said little. There was no need. There's something comfortable and comforting about being with someone you've lived more than half your life with. It's not that you don't think about the excitement you once shared when your relationship was fresh and new, what a walk along the beach would mean to you as a couple then. And it's not that older relationships don't still experience new phases, but I was enjoying the safety of knowing I knew this man better really than anyone knew him, and he knew me the same way.

In fact, I believe someone had perfectly designed him to stand alongside me as I worked through what I'd carried. I doubt there would be any others who could have withstood the changes I went through and the challenges that brought for him. It's a bit of an in-house joke, but he's often told me our life together has felt like being married to three different women.

And what of Paul? We're friends—good friends. No matter the distance of time or proximity, the relationship is the same. And that warm feeling of affirmation that used to turn me inside out, that's transformed, no longer accosting me when I feel someone's approval. What I experience now is a steady sense that I have something to add to this world, not greater or lesser, depending on the judgment of others.

It felt like freedom to be on the beach that day, just walking the dog. Yet, freedom had always seemed such an elusive state and I can only describe it in terms of what the moment wasn't. There was a time when to walk out onto that beach would have felt exposing and time restricted, as if something or someone I couldn't see was watching me or I needed to get back to something, yet I couldn't quite remember what. My dear friend Teri once told me a dream she'd had, about a black panther trailing my every move. It really was a fitting description, perhaps a vision of what I'd been driven by. I remember taking photos of a panther at a lion park, and in viewing the photos later, I noticed the animal had all but disappeared; only its yellow eyes remained visible. What I realised is the panther Teri told me about was no longer with me, its eyes no longer watching, the fear and the drive no longer present.

I remembered Beth, who had passed away prematurely, how she'd said that eventually this day would come. I'd be walking along; I'd look behind me and what had driven me would no longer be there. Had I believed her? No way I had. How could I have seen beyond where I was? Though I believed something, not that one day I would be free, that was too big, but I believed what God had told me. That Simone is "one who hears or one who listens." Even the story of how I got my name speaks to who I am; my mother lying in a hospital bed before giving birth, a mother in another bed calling out to her daughter Simone, and my mother deciding on hearing it, that the name would be mine. And eventually I heard God speak to me, not because there was anything special about me, but because of who He is, and my recognition of that enabled Him to tell me who I am (Matthew 16:15-18).

I had thought it would be more earth shattering to find I was free, the thing that had haunted me most of my life gone, but really it was just a nod, an acknowledgement that I'd made it. When I'd been on the uphill side, the desperation to get rid of it had never left me. It'd felt as if it would take a miracle to get there, and I think it did. But the incremental way I'd come to it meant there'd been nothing jarring about the result. And I'd come out the other side with so much more than just being free of what was following me. Freedom from that had been my small hope. What God had seen for me was a relationship with Him through Jesus. His way, His life; "... I am the way, and the truth, and the life; no one comes to the Father but through Me" (John 14:6). And it was He who'd brought me around to it, had orchestrated the whole thing. He was the composer.

But what I had seemed able to do during that process was to remember, but then only because I wrote it down, as if my natural state was or is to forget. That's in part why I'm fascinated by what the Israelites did whenever God said something to them or did something for them. They built altars. It was a memorial, a way of remembering what had passed between God and His people. During my battle, I had thought my way out had been Beth, or my relationship with Paul, or the many others who'd had an impact. That it was them, that they had been the key to my healing. But they'd been people faithful to the call of God in their lives as it related to me. My healer was God and Him alone.

I'd known very early in my journaling that I would write a book drawing from what I'd written. I didn't know the nature of it, only that I would write it, and now I see it's a memorial too. The word the prophet received for me said the complaint in my heart was my vision. It took a long time to work out what my complaint was. I think of the girl I was at the beginning of my story, so vulnerable to any attention, particularly masculine. How minor the incident in the marae was, yet because of a careless teaching from my mother a few years earlier, and the lack of engagement of my father, I set off on a destructive path. And my complaint? There was no one with any wisdom to stop me. No grandparent, aunt or uncle, no friend of the family. My parents didn't have what I needed, but I didn't blame them. It wasn't in them. But there was God, my Father in heaven. The prophet Tony Saxon had told me:

> I felt the Lord saying I am changing so much about who you are that you will define things differently in yourself, you will define things differently in your past, you will define things differently in your current situations because God has and will continue to refashion your mind ...

And He did. He took me back through my life, and He showed me where He was. I was never alone. And in Greg Burson's prophetic word, He told me:

> I think God has always been the one who shapes your providence ... Remember the word providence. It's kind of like Romans 8:28. He works everything together for good in a way that only He can understand, and I just hope that He puts you more and more in the picture ...

So, it's fitting that my story draws to a close with the words God spoke through Greg to inspire me to tell it:

> Tell your story. Tell people what you have coped with and carried, what you have worked through and what you have walked through and let that unfold in front of people and watch them be amazed at the goodness of God in a person's life.

Epilogue

2021

I'd told the ladies I wouldn't speak, feeling certain that if God had wanted me to, He'd have made it clear. It disappointed them. They wanted to hear what I had to say, but I didn't think they were ready—or maybe I wasn't ready for them to hear it. We were on a ladies' camp, all of us from the church I'd been attending for several years now, ever since we'd come back from Auckland. We were staying at a camping ground in an area I was painfully familiar with. I had history there.

A small group of us had arrived on the Friday night, and as we'd entered the hall, we'd found our name tags beautifully decorated and sitting on a table waiting to be collected. There were pretty lights strung on the cornices, artful scripture on the walls, fancy clothes we could choose to wear, or not, and delightful smells emanating from the kitchen down the end. Most of us were sleeping in bunkrooms through doors directly off the hall. We were only a third of the total number of attendees, though, as most were to arrive on Saturday morning.

Those first few hours of a camp are always the hardest, as everyone settles into their roles, and those who have been busy arranging things have yet to let themselves relax after the busyness of getting the event ready. I think it was surprising for the organisers to find there was so much help when we all arrived. We did the little jobs that the team hadn't been able to finish, and then all of us sat and chatted for hours. After supper, and an impromptu sing-along, we gradually drifted off to bed, eager to be fresh for when everyone else arrived the following day.

It unsettled everything when the ladies turned up the next morning, as they brought with them an energy and intensity we'd all put aside. It was then the event really launched, though. It started with worship and then we heard from the speaker, followed by lunch, and then in the afternoon we were free to do what we wanted. That was the point at which my connection to the location raised its head.

There were several suggested options of how we might spend the afternoon, but a friend from home group asked if I'd care to take a walk with her. I felt like some exercise, and it was a lovely day, so we headed off up the steep climb to the main road. My friend wanted to see the house she'd lived in when she first arrived in New Zealand. I did sense I was about to be confronted by my past, but I didn't really get to dwell on it as she chatted away about her arrival in the country, and what that had been like for her.

As she led me down a road towards her old house, I suspected, though I wasn't entirely sure, that we were on the same road I'd driven down some thirty years earlier, searching for the house Joey lived in. He was the man I'd had the affair with in my teen years. The road was longer than I remembered, which kept me guessing, but as we got close to the end, my friend pointed out the house she'd brought me to see. Of course, I recognised the area, and surprise, surprise, the house my friend had lived in was right next door to where Joey had lived all those years ago. What were the chances of that?

I knew the moment was spiritually significant, though my friend was oblivious to what I was experiencing, and I let her remain so. She chatted on about this and that and I tried to stay engaged while still connecting to what was going on for me. It felt heavy, not in a bad way, more the Holy Spirit was brooding, clearly wanting to gain my attention, and He had it.

We continued our walking circuit along the beach and when we got back to the main hall, I made a beeline for my bunkroom to gather my thoughts before heading down to the prayer room, set up in a private lounge overlooking the bay. When I got there, there was another lady taking advantage of the quietness, but not long after I arrived, she left. I'd never been much of a one for prayer rooms, thinking that you prayed where you were, but I had to admit, with the worship music playing, the candles, the scripture and artwork placed around the room, I was fast being converted. I felt the familiar drop into the Spirit, and I stayed communing quietly for a time, before heading back into the melee in the main hall. I don't think I expected anything more to come of it.

The evening was raucous and fun, with a lovely meal and a competitive fashion show, and then I began looking forward to Sunday as I knew the numbers would drop again, and things would get personal, intimate, just the way I liked it.

Sunday morning was subdued, particularly when compared to the previous night. I recognised the feeling. It was reverence, almost as if we were all waiting on something, a sense of presence we hoped would grace us. This was the moment the ladies asked me to speak, and I declined.

So, the session began, the planned speakers taking their turns. Then they made it open mic, and a couple of ladies got up. As they spoke, I could feel the Spirit pressing me, and I became aware I was to go next. The Lord was drawing me, and He was not to be denied.

The emcee held the mic out, offering it to anyone, and I leant forward, pushing myself out of my seat.

"Oh, Simone?" I heard, as those who knew I'd said no to speaking, expressed their surprise.

I hadn't wanted to think too much about what I was going to say. God had prompted me. I believed He would give me the words, and He did. I told them about my walk with my friend the day before, about being led to the house I'd gone to so many years earlier, as a newly married woman, in search of the man I'd had the affair with. How the boy had walked across the road in front of my car, and I'd recognised his eyes, known that he was Joey's son, and that all I'd seen in those eyes was accusation.

I told the ladies I realized why this had happened now, on this weekend, in this place. I knew what it was all about, what the Spirit wanted me to understand. He wanted me to tell my story. It was Him who'd prompted me to speak to them, I'd not intended to. He'd told me over ten years earlier to tell my story, and now He was confirming His word. Two or three witnesses. He was highlighting it, affirming and releasing me, and His presence was incredible.

When I'd finished, I went back to my seat, and although the women had been impacted by my story, I felt they were unaware of the strength of the Lord's presence, certainly the way I was experiencing it. And maybe it had to be that way. After all, it was me who had received the commissioning, me who had been told to tell my story, that He would cause it to be a great demonstration of the gospel, so I was the one who needed to step into my calling.

And so here I am, here it is. If you're reading this, I've done it. Of course, I realise I may never see the roaring I was told I would do, that it may come after I'm gone. And the book might only reach one person—you.

But I believe the word my Great Grandfather left, that what he heard in the Spirit applies:

> I took God to the best spots in my garden, but God wanted to see the results of all my efforts, saying they didn't matter, "that is not your concern ... none of my children have weedless gardens or perfect fruit. Come, we will walk together to the darkest spots, and perhaps some good may come of it."

Sidney Clayton, 18 January 1952

Acknowledgements

Thank you to those who encouraged and helped me along the way. They include, but are not limited to, Katharine Hemingway who went home way too soon, to Teri Meyer, to mum, and both of my oh so patient and wise mentors who I know would not like to be named. To Ruth Gillingham, Liz Croft, Dianne Holwell, Hilary Beath, Chelc Smart, Craig Gemmell, and Helen Aoina who all put in the hard yards of going through my manuscript. To the kindhearted pastor who was the right person, in the right place at the right time, to our precious Aussie brother and sister (faith is the key), and finally to my ever patient and forgiving husband Steve and our joy boy Elijah, thank you. You've all blessed me beyond measure with your presence in my life.

Bibliography

Allender, Dan B. & Longman III, Tremper. (1994). *Cry of the Soul: How Our Emotions Reveal Our Deepest Questions About God.* NavPress. Colorado Springs.

Eldredge, John. (2000). *The Journey of Desire: Searching for the Life We've Only Dreamed Of.* Thomas Nelson Publishers. Tennessee.

Marshall, G. (director). (2004). *Raising Helen* [Film]. Touchstone Pictures.

May, Gerald. G. (1988). *Addiction and Grace.* HarperCollins Publishers. New York.

May, Gerald. G. (2004). *The Dark Night of the Soul: A Psychiatrist Explores the Connection Between Darkness and Spiritual Growth.* HarperCollins Publishers. New York.

Rainer, Tristine. (1997). *Your Life as Story: Discovering The "New Autobiography" And Writing Memoir as Literature.* Penguin Putnam Inc. New York.

Roberts, Monty. (2023, January 23). *Monty Roberts: A Real Horse Whisperer.* [Video]. YouTube. https://www.youtube.com/watch?v=H8NEekz1Ij4

Zondervan (Author), Ronald A. Beers (Editor). New American Standard Bible: Life Application Study Bible. (2000). p.456.